Interviews with William Carlos Williams

"Speaking Straight Ahead"

For Florence H. Williams

By William Carlos Williams

The Autobiography
The Build-up
Collected Earlier Poems
Collected Later Poems
The Embodiment of Knowledge
The Farmers' Daughters
I Wanted to Write a Poem*
Imaginations
In the American Grain
In the Money
Kora in Hell: Improvisations†
Many Loves and Other Plays
Paterson, Books 1–5
Pictures from Brueghel and Other Poems
The Selected Essays
Selected Poems
A Voyage to Pagany
White Mule
The William Carlos Williams Reader

* *Beacon Press*
† *City Lights Books*

Interviews with William Carlos Williams

"Speaking Straight Ahead"

edited with an introduction by
Linda Welshimer Wagner

A NEW DIRECTIONS BOOK

Grateful acknowledgment is made to the editors and publishers of periodicals and books where some of the material in this volume first appeared: *American Scholar*, *Ann Arbor Review*, *A. D.*, *The Golden Goose*, Beacon Press for William Carlos Williams's *I Wanted to Write A Poem*, ed. Edith Heal, *The Massachusetts Review*, *Mica 3*, *The Minnesota Review*, *New Directions in Prose and Poetry 1936*, *New Directions in Prose and Poetry 17*, *New York Post*, *The New York Times Book Review*, *Paris Review* (and The Viking Press, which included the interview with William Carlos Williams in *Writers at Work: The Paris Review Interviews*, Copyright © 1967 by The Paris Review, Inc.), *Partisan Review*, *Paterson Morning Call*, Cambridge University Press for *William Carlos Williams, The American Background* by Mike Weaver.

The editor also wishes to thank the following publishers and individuals for permission to reprint from copyrighted sources: Golden Goose Press, Columbus, Ohio, for material from *The Golden Goose*, No. 3, June 1949 (Copyright 1949 by Richard Wirtz Emerson) and *The Golden Goose*, Series 3, No. 2 (Copyright 1951 by Golden Goose Press); Frederick Eckman for lines from his poem "Hagiography" (Copyright © 1967, 1970 by Frederick Eckman); *New York Post* for excerpts from "Is Poetry a Dead Duck?" an interview by Mike Wallace (Copyright © 1957 by New York Post Corporation); and *The New York Times* for portions of "Talk with William Carlos Williams" by Harvey Breit (Copyright 1950 by The New York Times Company).

Special thanks are due as well to Mrs. John C. Thirwall for permission to use excerpts from the tapes her husband made of conversations with Dr. Williams; to Gael Turnbull for allowing the editor to reprint a section of his diary; and to the Collection of American Literature, Beinecke Rare Book and Manuscript Library, Yale University, for permission to use manuscript material.

Manufactured in the United States of America
First published clothbound and as New Directions Paperbook 421 in 1976
Published simultaneously in Canada by McClelland & Stewart, Ltd.

Library of Congress Cataloging in Publication Data

Williams, William Carlos, 1883–1963.
Interviews with William Carlos Williams: "Speaking straight ahead."
(A New Directions Book)
Includes bibliographical references and index.
1. Williams, William Carlos, 1883–1963—Interviews.
I. Wagner, Linda Welshimer. II. Title.
PS3545.I544Z526 1976 818'.5'209[B] 76-14797
ISBN 0-8112-0620-3
ISBN 0-8112-0621-1 pbk.

New Directions Books are published for James Laughlin by New Directions Publishing Corporation,
333 Sixth Avenue, New York 10014

Contents

III. MEMOIR AND MISCELLANY

Introduction

"Speaking Straight Ahead . . ."

William Carlos Williams said it when he was seventy-eight, when—after several strokes and other illnesses—he could hardly speak. But the phrase is apt for both his exuberant, staccato delivery (the voice high and rushed, almost breathless) and the impetuous yet strangely hesitant intelligence behind it. For Williams, speech was identity. He had listened carefully through a lifetime to the diction and the inflection of his patients, his friends, his culture; he had used language signals as a means of making diagnoses; most important of all, he had based his own poetics on theories of speech rhythms:

> The rhythmical construction of a poem was determined for me by the language as it is spoken. Word of mouth language, not classical English.
>
> (*I Wanted to Write a Poem*, p. 75)

For the earnest young doctor of Rutherford, poetry was his most important activity. He was a pediatrician, yes; he loved being a pediatrician (and a general practitioner as well. Sixty years ago a doctor was a doctor, no matter what his speciality); and his care for his patients surfaces often in both his fiction and his poems. But Williams knew, early, that he wanted a literary life. He worked as a physician so that he might write what he chose, free from any kind of financial or political pressure. From the beginning, in the early 1900s, he understood the trade-offs: he would have less time to write; he would need more physical stamina than people with only one occupation; he would probably demand more from his family. But Williams, with the help of his wife, the remarkable Flossie, was willing to live the kind of rushed existence that would be necessary, crowding two full lifetimes into one, juggling experience and meditation, learning from the first and then understanding through the second.

> . . . my "medicine" was the thing which gained me entrance to these secret gardens of the self. It lay there, another world, in the self. I was permitted by my medical badge to follow the poor, defeated body into those gulfs and grottos.
>
> (*Autobiography*, p. 288)

Judging from his more than forty published books, from his position today as one of our most innovative and generous modern writers, we must conclude that Williams's sometimes frantic lifestyle did work successfully. For him. For him, then. That lifestyle, however, can hardly be considered a paradigm for every writer who wants to succeed; perhaps it is more a tribute to Williams's own tough will that he saw its risks and still made it. But it may be that the combination of careers worked for him at least partly because it was in basic agreement with Williams's personal aesthetic position, even in the groping years when he scarcely had one.

Contact with people—happy people, troubled people, excited and nervous people—meant contact with language. Williams's most consistent principle in sixty years of writing was the use of natural speech rhythms, the line divided and spaced so as to suggest rhythmic breaks in the language as spoken. His hatred of prescribed forms like the sonnet and the influence of formal, British English stems from the same root: he considered such formality inimical to American English. "And the guys from Paterson beat up the guys from Newark, and told them to stay the hell out of their territory," lines from "Paterson: Episode 17," would never fit into an Italian sonnet. No way. So Williams chose to stay with what he was convinced *were* the true materials of his art—American people, American life—

and create a poetics that could accommodate his multiple subjects. As he reminisced about *Al Que Quiere:*

> The poems are for the most part short, written in conversational language as spoken . . . . the sheer sense of what is spoken seemed to me all important . . . . From this time on you can see the struggle to get a form without deforming the language.
> (*I Wanted* . . . , p. 22)

"To get a form without deforming the language"—an accurate description of the last forty years of Williams's craft. During the 1930s, he turned to poems which were simply fragments of idiom:

Vhy'n't you bring me
good letter? One with
ts of money in it.
could make use of that.
tta boy! Atta boy!

Hi, open up a dozen.

What'cha tryin' ta do—
charge ya batteries?

Make it two.

Easy girl!
you'll blow a fuse if
ya keep that up.

Hey!
Can I have some more milk?

YEEEEAAAAASSSSS!
—always the gentle
mother!

These idiomatic poems led Williams toward the whole performance of *Paterson,* his five-book treatise on the aesthetic problem of getting a form without deforming the language, as well as recording his own search for an expressive language ("Strike in! the middle of / some trenchant phrase, some / well packed clause . . .").

Paterson is that remarkable mixture of poetry and prose, loose-lined poems cut by shorter-lined tercets, quasi-formal rhetoric, a section of verse play, and—superimposed—the montage of quotations from stodgy histories of Paterson, notes, and impassioned letters from other struggling writers. A hodgepodge, the American version of Pound's more famous "ragbag," *Paterson* grew from Williams's need to express his fascination with country/man/language; to put it all together instead of fragmenting it—this huge, stirring emotional nexus—so that it would fit into the tidy poems that he was then writing. *Paterson*'s creation, section by section, book by book, is recorded clearly —and painfully—in the collections of Williams's papers at both the Yale and Buffalo libraries: hundreds of drafted pages and as many notes, never used. The history of *Paterson* is a series of false starts, of unexpected stops. But finally, casting out on his own just as Pound did with the *Cantos* and Melville did with *Moby-Dick*, Williams trusted only to his constant and enduring principle: "the colloquial language, my own language, set the pace."

Amazing—Williams and the writing of this five-book poem. Completely abjuring any traditional form or genre, he began with what were for him central thematic issues —marriage and divorce, virtue, modern life, and man's search through it all for "a redeeming language":

Say it, no ideas but in things.

What common language to unravel?

a confession . . . hard put to it

The language, the language/fails them/
They know not the words/or have not/
the courage to use them.

With those amorphous principles, he somehow wrestled from an already bewildering lifetime of experience (the quantity of materials he wanted to include is staggering in itself) a few characters, selected scenes, chary images to create the effective poem. But in the process of writing, he confronted again and again the problem of using real speech so that it was more than local color. There was a great difference between Williams's concept of "using" speech, of *finding* the character through his speech, and of just mixing in flavorful slang or idiom as relief in more formal poetic diction. Here is the most important difference, I believe, between Williams and poets like Vachel Lindsay, Sandburg, Cummings, the earlier Eliot, and even

Whitman who—for all his interest in the American character—always managed to write in the same heavily traditional vocabulary.

For Williams, any person's identity rested on his spoken language. Many of his short stories open with a character speaking; we hear the words with no introduction or setting given:

> There were a coupla guys prowling around down here this morning but when they seen me they beat it.
>
> ("The Dawn of Another Day")

> Which is "the black day"? he asked her.
>
> ("The Cold World")

> "He's asleep."
>
> ("Four Bottles of Beer")

In *Paterson*, Williams continues this tactic of preserving natural speech. Whole pages from letters he had received appear unchanged in the poem; speech here, through arrangement, is raised to art. Earlier, in the Cotton Mather section of *In the American Grain*, Williams had used the same approach, by letting Mather's own language and phrasing "create" his personality. The device, for Williams, was not new. In his poetry, however, because of the intrinsic formal differences between poetry and prose, his reliance on this speech identity took on a new ramification. As he pointed out,

> The rhythmic unit usually came to me in a lyrical outburst. I wanted it to look that way on the page. I didn't go in for long lines because of my nervous nature. I couldn't. The rhythmic pace was the pace of speech, an excited pace because I was excited when I wrote.
>
> (*I Wanted . . .*, p. 15)

Speech as the origin of form, of shape: set against T. S. Eliot's very moderate view of a poet's use of tradition, Williams explodes: "A false language. A true. A false language pouring—a language (misunderstood) pouring (misinterpreted) without dignity. . . ."

It is not that Williams opted entirely for innovation. Pound chanted "Make it new" for sixty years; Williams's parallel cry was "the American language." As Williams wrote, "Free verse was not the answer. From the beginning, I knew that the American language must shape the pattern." And the way this whole process occurs, Williams describes in the 1944 "Introduction" to *The Wedge:*

> . . . its movement is intrinsic, undulant, a physical more than a literary character. In a poem this movement is distinguished . . . by the character of the speech from which it arises.

In his famous description of the poem as a machine, from the same introduction, he continues to stress the crucial importance of the language, speech. The poetic act begins there, in speech, with the poet serving as listener:

> When a man makes a poem, makes it, mind you, he takes words as he finds them *interrelated about him* [italics added] and composes them . . . . that they may constitute a revelation in the speech that he uses.

Significant here is the notion that the words are active, in use, "interrelated about him." The poet is not isolated with a thesaurus, playing verbal games, making puns and anagrams; the poet is he who walks through life, listening, being involved, participating more than watching. Literature is filled with observer-artists, but no one could ever accuse Williams of being withdrawn. He is rather the poet of the sensual, and especially the poet of the ear, since his whole poetics depended upon his interest in inflection and idiom.

But Williams was looking for more than a technical ploy, and perhaps that is another reason his insistence on the use of the natural idiom is important. For he was throughout his life, even though he fought Wallace Stevens's designation, a great Romantic.

All this–
was for you, old woman.
I wanted to write a poem
that you would understand . . . .

And he did. Williams really wanted to reach a public, a public at least partly comprised of actual people, and part of his anger with the academic establishment resulted from its ignoring him. (If no one anthologized his poems, how were the common readers to find them?) Williams wanted to reach people because he saw so many sterile, impoverished lives: poetry, art, beauty might somehow ease those terrors. It was no whim: he believed it early in his career; he believed it at the end of his life, writing in "Asphodel,"

It is difficult
to get the news from poems
yet men die miserably every day
for lack
of what is found there.
Hear me out
for I too am concerned
and every man
who wants to die at peace in his bed
besides.

The theme occurs over and over in Williams's poems: he sees the poem as a way to self-knowledge, the poem as a means of reaching, of communicating, of–in simple–speaking. "Would it disturb you if I said," he wrote early in "Writer's Prologue to a Play in Verse," "you have no other speech than poetry?" And later in the poem, he says it plainly, that he is aiming to help his reader find "the undiscovered language of yourself."

In *The Autobiography* too Williams spends much time on the somewhat Jungian process of finding oneself through language:

> The physician enjoys a wonderful opportunity actually to witness words being born . . . . Nothing is more moving.

But after we have run the gamut of simple meanings that come to one over the years, a change gradually occurs. We have grown used to the range of communication which is likely to reach us . . . . then a new meaning begins to intervene. For under that language to which we have been listening all our lives a new, a more profound language, underlying all dialectics, offers itself. It is what they call poetry . . . ."

(*The Autobiography*, p. 361)

As poet or as doctor, Williams was fascinated with "the poem that each is trying actually to communicate to us." To his credit, he heard, unearthed, a good many of those inarticulate poems, and he made new shapes where none existed before, to embody the particular—and particularly American—beauties of his townspeople and their language.

These same concerns occur repeatedly in the spoken interviews themselves. Williams was not often interviewed, since fame came late to him, and all figures of history who tie themselves to a single location know how begrudging—and tardy—the small town is with its laurels. But whenever he did have the chance to speak for public record, his enthusiasm, his boundless energy dominate the interchange. "Yes, yes!" he answers vehemently when the interviewer phrases something well. And, of his friendship with Ezra Pound, "Wasn't that marvelous though!" and "Never! Never worked with him at all in anything! Never have had any task that I know of in common (except to reform the American nation and the world, incidentally—of course that's a small matter), but [*laughs*] between the two of us, we'd like to uproot poetry and start it on its own, on its proper tracks in this country. [*laughs*]" This brief excerpt from a 1950 interview shows clearly Williams's proclivity for hyperbole, his ironic humor, his sheer enjoyment of his role, the latter illustrated by his frequent chuckles, even laughter. As Harvey Breit wrote in his 1950 *New York Times* portrait,

The following judgment is made in all honesty and with due consideration: the sixty-six-year-old poet and pediatrician, William Carlos Williams, has more intellectual *vitality* than any poet or two pediatricians this side of the Atlantic. Dr. Williams, tall and bony, with graying hair, and whose bold features have been softened a little by his labors with humans as well as with the humanities, speaks with spectacular vigor on subjects ranging from art to zoology, in a voice that subtly twangs with cosmic impatience.

These same characteristics of enthusiasm, vigor, and spontaneity mark much of Williams's written essays too, and have led some critics to call his prose "contradictory," "uneven." A good many years ago, Emerson had the definitive word on consistency, but Williams added a postscript to that in 1944, already feeling the repercussions from a lifetime of eager speaking and writing:

> A man isn't a block that remains stationary, though the psychologists treat him so . . . . Consistency! He varies; Hamlet today, Caesar tomorrow; here, there, somewhere—if he is to retain his sanity.

Against the impression that he was sometimes careless, let us set the image that Williams would have himself approved, that of a devoted artist, aware that time was running out, *urgently* trying to get it all said, to move everyone he cared about to the point of acceptance; and that persuasion took energy, took time. If one tack didn't work, he would try another (to hell with the wasted first attempt. Williams was never one to sit and sulk). If one argument didn't convince, surely, somewhere, there existed one that would. (Some of the greatest sorrows of his later life were the evidences of closed minds around him—Yvor Winters's sudden and, to Williams, inexplicable shift from being a supporter to a critic, Sandburg's apparent refusal to attempt anything "new" in many years, Pound's stubborn political stance.)

It is true that Williams's aesthetic position was created at least partly from flashes of insight instead of careful stepping from one well-defined position to the next. Recent critics like Anthony Libby and Ron Loewinsohn have defended his method as being ultralogical, more reasonable perhaps than the formalized procedures of recent centuries, but Williams himself felt hesitant; and his own rushed, headlong speech pattern is in some ways a reflection of that tension between commitment assured and confident, and commitment under constant if surreptitious scrutiny. That he was for most of his career a man under attack is not news to anyone familiar with the criticism of his work. Many academics found it hard to accept a man who could declare so positively, "The American idiom has much to offer us that the English language has never heard of."

> We were speaking straight ahead about what concerned us, and if I could have overheard what I was saying then, that would have given me a hint of how to phrase myself, to say what I had to say. Not after the establishment, but speaking straight ahead. I would gladly have traded what I have tried to say, for what came off my tongue, naturally.
>
> (*Paris Review*)

Whether he was speaking to the book editor of *The New York Times*, to Robert Frost, to other doctors, to the ladies' groups of Rutherford, to younger writers, or to patients, Williams said what he had to say. His plain speaking cost him ground politically (Flossie recalls in the *Paris Review* interview that Williams was often embroiled in controversy: "He's an honest man. And if he gets into it with both feet, it's just too bad"), but it won for him the reputation of candor and trust that made him the patron saint of so many younger writers. It was Williams who told Ginsberg that "Howl" needed cutting by half; it was Williams who argued with Denise Levertov about her sometimes too-poetic diction; but it was also Williams who gave countless writers the encouragement and confidence to continue their own work. As Gael Turnbull recalls, "It was as if he had opened his mind to you completely, every disconnected fragment that came into his mind." They trusted him, those eternally alienated artists of the forties and fifties; and the qualities of his speaking that remained most often with them were his honesty and, in equal part, his gentle, old-fashioned compassion. It is the latter quality Frederick Eckman catches in "Hagiography":

> And that loving man William Williams,
> parish priest of all objects living,
> will find in heaven wheelbarrows, plums:
> all that is required for perfect joy.

And for Williams, his own perfect joy came from the thrill of accurately catching his people, in their own language, and in a poetry that opened *form* and *genre* to all kinds of experimentation. It could well be that in the future, Williams will be compared more often with those other great innovators of modern American literature—Stein, Hemingway, Dos Passos—than with his fellow "poets." And perhaps that will be just as well, for "speaking" in itself knows no *genre* distinctions. It is an act of voice —a human act—and its purpose is, and has always been, to reach.

July 1, 1976 LINDA WELSHIMER WAGNER
East Lansing, Michigan

I
Interviews

The three interviews with William Carlos Williams reprinted in their entirety here create the indelible stamp of the poet's candor and enthusiasm. The 1950 interview, recorded by John W. Gerber and edited in 1973 by Emily M. Wallace, is reprinted from *The Massachusetts Review, XIV*, No. 1 (Winter 1973). The second interview, "The Editors Meet William Carlos Williams," is narrative in style rather than being a literal transcription. Written by Dorothy Tooker, the piece appeared in Volume III, No. 1 of *A.D.* (the A. D. Literary Association), Winter of 1952. The last, Walter Sutton's 1961 interview, was published in *The Minnesota Review*, I, in 1961.

An Interview with William Carlos Williams

John W. Gerber and Emily M. Wallace

John W. Gerber, the interviewer, visited William Carlos Williams at the handsome old house on 9 Ridge Road by appointment on a rainy June afternoon in 1950, probably Sunday, June 18. There was no rehearsal or preliminary to the interview other than a reading of the poem "This Is Just to Say," to test the recording equipment, nor were any questions submitted in advance. Gerber had prepared carefully, and Williams was so responsive to Gerber's questions and spoke so effortlessly that in less than an hour the interview was completed, the final word trailing off at the end of the tape, a perfect exit.

The weather that June day a quarter of a century ago was gloomy and dark, Gerber remembers, but Williams's mood was not. It was an ideal time in Williams's life for an interview. The previous year in May he had written to a friend, "I really want to loosen myself up for the final sprint to the finish." Then in August to another friend, he had said, "I am more than ever convinced that my own career has been one long mistake," but in the following months, besieged by honors, praise, and publicity, his mood swung upward. Early in 1950 he was elected to the National Institute of Arts and Letters, and the National Book Award was given to his *Selected Poems* and Book Three of *Paterson.* Photographers from *Time* and *Life* insisted upon pictures. Invitations from colleges and universities were pouring in. His play *A Dream of Love* had been presented in New York the previous summer, and someone in Hollywood was negotiating to make a movie of it. He had written a catalog note for a Picasso show, and was working on the libretto for an opera with Ben Weber. New Directions was preparing a new edition of his collected poems and waiting for Book Four of *Paterson.* Random House was preparing an edition of his collected short stories and waiting for his autobiography and a novel. Although he had in 1948 suffered a heart attack, his health at this time was good. His two sons, safely home from the war, were married and living in Rutherford, Paul working as a business executive in New York, and William Eric as "a diplomate in pediatrics," according to his father, "who is fast robbing me of my medical practice, much to my delight." New babies, his own grandchildren, had arrived or were on the way, also much to his delight. He had also had to accept deaths in the family;

his mother had died in October of the previous year, and his wife's mother in December. At this point in his life, the precarious balancing in his subtle mind of respect for the past and reverence for new beginnings had reached a fine equilibrium. Like Odysseus, asked to tell his story on his homeward voyage from Troy, Williams willingly recalls past struggles and triumphs and looks forward to the journey before him, or, as he had said, "the final sprint to the finish."

Williams never heard the entire interview after it was over or saw a text of it. If he had edited the text himself, the result might have demonstrated his passion for succinctness. The uncut version reveals other qualities, such as an unexpected expansiveness in talking about the past, his generosity in explaining and clarifying, and his dutiful, if impatient, mention of other views of a problem while making the clean thrust straight through to his solution.

Williams's voice on the tape is youthful (he was then sixty-seven) and vibrant, a musical tenor very expressive of his earnest reflection or courteous indignation or outrageous irony. As always, he is involved in the present moment, even though it be the act of remembrance. Recalling a child in distress (himself), his voice breaks on the word "distress"; speaking of his wife Flossie, his voice becomes touchingly gentle; repeating the words of Dr. Calhoun or Bunk Johnson or "some Englishman," he dramatizes the different rhythms of speech. Often, the tone of voice expresses his amusement at the whole proceeding of talking about himself. "The sign of a poet's unforgiving seriousness is his rebellious laughter," he wrote in 1919, and frequent laughter is an important part of this 1950 interview. It ranges from joyful chuckles, in remembering ol' Ez or something Flossie had said, to a kind of merry sigh, at once rebellious and apologetic, before or after a statement of ponderable value, as if to signal that the statement is (or is not) a serious one to be (or not to be) taken seriously.

The following text of this 1950 interview is presented with the assistance and permission of John W. Gerber, Ruth E. Koehler, Gladys Eckardt, Director of The Free Public Library of Rutherford, and Florence H. Williams. The text is based on the acetate discs made by Jack Gerber from the original tapes, which subsequently were destroyed. Shortly after Williams's death in March of 1963, Ruth Koehler, of Rutherford, transcribed the interview from the original tapes given to her by Gerber, and from copies of them. With Miss Koehler's immensely helpful typescript before me, I listened to several generations of recordings, working mainly from the youngest, a cassette that was made from the two duplicate tapes in the Rutherford library (each tape contains a few words not on the other), which are copies of the acetate discs. Jack Gerber thoughtfully gave me the acetate discs for the final check of the accuracy of the text. I have not rearranged or cut the interview, except to omit some repetitive phrases and false starts. The punctuation is based on the emphases of Williams's spoken voice.—Emily M. Wallace

INTERVIEWER: What I had in mind was simply having you talk about the problems of being a doctor and being a poet–

WILLIAMS: Oh. Yes, I see.

INTERVIEWER:–and perhaps start by telling how you got to be a doctor and a poet.

WILLIAMS: Hmmn. Well you want me to begin way back [*laughs*].

INTERVIEWER: Begin way back.

WILLIAMS: Well all right, I was born–that's where we begin usually–born right in Rutherford of parents who were themselves born out of the country. My father [1] was born in England and didn't come here till he was brought here by his mother, having lost his father at the age of five. And, well, switch to Mother,[2] she was born in Mayagüez, Puerto Rico, of mixed parentage she was, her mother coming originally from Martinique, a Frenchwoman, and her father being a Puerto Rican. So, they came here. My father came here because the advantages there for a young man going into business were not great, came to New York, moved to Rutherford, and here I was born–[*laughs*] that's the way it begins. I have one brother.[3] We were both born here.

When it came to a decision about what I should do in life to earn a living, which was of course very distasteful to me that I should have to earn a living, it was very very bad [*laughs*]. Never having had anything, it was quite natural that I should continue doing nothing [*laughs*] and still having nothing–I thought it would be all right. Well, my middle name is Carlos. My mother had one brother who was her *beau idéal*. He was Carlos too. He was her only brother, as I say, who became a physician, graduated from the University of Paris, and started to practice in the West Indies and became rather a good surgeon, and I was named after him, so that, well, I was rather pushed into medicine rather than choosing it myself. My own choice was to be a forester, strange to say. Yeah. I had no desire to be among people. I lived rather a solitary sort of life with one or two companions. I liked to be outdoors and had no intention of becoming a physician, at all.

I went to Horace Mann High School in New York City. My brother and I commuted from here, taking the 7:16 train every morning for the three years that I went there, taking the Chambers Street ferry, walking up Chambers or Warren Street, taking the Sixth or Ninth Avenue El, riding up to 116th or 125th Street, and walking up Morningside Heights, and getting to Horace Mann High School on Morningside Heights in time for the nine o'clock bell. That was quite a little stunt. The reason for connecting that up is that I'd been very athletic. I was never any good at anything, but I loved it, and that's what I wanted to do, to be outdoors and to go into baseball and track. And I went into track a little bit too much, without a coach. I remember that I was going to run in Madison Square Garden a 300-yard run. That's a queer distance, just between the 220 and the quarter mile. It was a handicap event and I was tutored to win it, if I ran according to my style and in my own class. And we were training at the 22nd Regiment Armory, and I ran around, put my sprint on at the end of the quarter mile, and then when we got to the end of it, somebody said, "You got one more lap to go," which was not bright. And being ambitious, I ran and probably continued my sprint all the way around, and came home sick at my stomach, with a headache, and was put to bed after that. And that knocked me out. I remember Dr. [Charles] Calhoun, our old family physician, said, "Well, you got a bad heart? You'll never be able to do anything but take long walks in the country."

All this is important because it determined my life thereafter, not to go into athletics or to do anything strenuous. And I had to give up forestry, the idea of being outdoors, and Mother said, "Well, why don't you become"—not a doctor yet, that hadn't come up—"be a dentist?" So I got into the University of Pennsylvania and enrolled for a course, a five-year course, by which I was to get two degrees, the D.D.S. of dentistry and the M.D. of medicine, and go into oral surgery, which was a bright idea [*laughs*]. After the first year of the combined course, I quit dentistry and went on with medicine, and so, largely because of my mother's remembrance of her brother who was a distinguished surgeon, and because there I was, I didn't know what else to do, and it was put into my head, I became a doctor. Lucky, too, for me, because it forced me to get used to people of all sorts, which was a fine thing for a writer or a potential writer.

INTERVIEWER: It was at Pennsylvania that you started writing poetry, wasn't it?

WILLIAMS: No, I had started before that. I had started a short time before that. I wrote—not poetry and I never pretended that I was writing poetry—I was interested in writing. I kept notebooks. I remember it must have been twenty-three (it may have gone up to twenty-eight because eight and three are somewhat alike, and I can't remember them as between twenty-three and twenty-eight) notebooks, and I wrote my immortal thoughts in those books [*laughs*], whatever they were. If I had an opinion about things about me, I'd jot it down, and occasionally it would take the loose form of verse. I was reading Keats at the time. Keats was my favorite.

INTERVIEWER: This was while you were still in Horace Mann?

WILLIAMS: While I was getting through, yes. I had some very good English teachers at Horace Mann. There was an Uncle Billy Abbott, who later went to Smith I think, one of the Abbott family of New York, the Lyman Abbotts and others—I don't know who the original was, but they were very interesting people. And I believe that Uncle Billy Abbott [4] was the first one who really led me toward English, toward writing, toward the satisfaction of externalizing my sorrows and distresses. And believe me, that's the way writing often starts, a disaster or a catastrophe of some sort, as happened to me, and you're a child not knowing where to go or what to do or what to think. He's thrown back so much on himself that he's really in distress. And if someone can teach him, through an art or through an interest in whatever it may be, to externalize his sorrows [*laughs*], like *The Sorrows of Werther*, he immediately is put on a good basis for life, if he can continue it. And I think that's the basis for my continued interest in writing, because by writing I rescue myself under all sorts of conditions, whatever it may be that has upset me or some trouble that I've got myself into [*laughs*] through my excessive energy, let's say, if there is any at times, then I can write and it relieves the feeling of distress. I think quite literally, psychologically, speaking as Freud might think [*laughs*], that writing has meant that to me all the way through.

I started to write! I even remember the first thing I ever wrote, because it was a sudden . . . it was a crisis. It was shortly after I had been forbidden to go into athletics, told that I shouldn't undertake anything too strenuous in life. I spontaneously said to myself:

A black black cloud
flew over the sun
driven by fierce flying
rain.

Well, immediately I thought, "That's the most stupid thing I've ever said because, after all, the rain doesn't drive the clouds," so at the same moment I was born a poet and a critic instantly [*laughs*]. And I've never forgotten either one. But the outstanding thing was that when I said that, I experienced a pleasure, a real pleasure, a delightful feeling as if I had done something outstanding. I had no idea what I'd done. I did plenty [*laughs*]—ruined myself for life! [*laughs*] From being a regular guy, I became a poet, that horrible thing! But it was a satisfaction, and it's continued ever since.

INTERVIEWER: You were with Pound at the University of Pennsylvania, weren't you?

WILLIAMS: Well, yes, yes, that's the next step in this eventful history. I went there. This, by the way, is all to be in my autobiography, which I have been commissioned by Random House to present to them in manuscript form on the first of March. I don't know whether I'm infringing any agreement with them, but after all, I'm talking about myself, and there's nothing private about that, God knows, [*laughs*] I hope.

Well, I went to Penn. I, fortunately for me, matriculated in both medicine and dentistry, so that at the end of that year I could go on with medicine, otherwise I'd have been stuck. I happened to have a room in the dormitories, which was next to that occupied by a man from St. Louis named Van Cleve. I don't remember his first name. I played the violin by the way, a little bit. Badly. Oh God, was I awful! [*laughs*] But I enjoyed it. Van Cleve, though, was a major in music with Professor Clarke, Dr. Clarke.[5] And he had a grand piano in his dormitory room, which is somewhat unusual, and he was *right* next to me. Fortunately I enjoyed music, otherwise I couldn't have stood it. Well it was just the wall between us, so we immediately became acquainted, and I told him that I wasn't interested in music, but I was interested in writing and somewhat in painting too. "Well, if you're interested in writing," he said, "there's a man in our class, he's a crazy guy, but I think you two would get along marvelously together. I'll bring him around some day."

So I said, "Go ahead, I'd like to meet some people that would be interesting." So whom should he bring?—but old Ez [*laughs*] . . . staggered up the stairs [*laughs*]. I don't remember that though. I don't remember the first meeting at all. But it just took one look, and I knew he was it![6] We have been intimate friends for the last, well, what is it? It's forty-eight years, that's a long time. We don't always get along together, and I don't approve of his attitude in many things, but basically his has been one of the most outstanding friendships that I've ever enjoyed. And I say *enjoyed* too, because you know as with any friend or member of the family, what you'd really like to do is pok'em one in the snoot—that means you love them [*laughs*]. You don't have to go along with him at all. In fact, I don't.

INTERVIEWER: Did you work with him at all in Paris?

WILLIAMS: Never! Never worked with him at all in anything! Never have had any task that I know of in common (except to reform the American nation and the world, incidentally—of course that's a small matter), but [*laughs*] between the two of us, we'd like to uproot poetry and start it on its own, on its proper tracks in this country. [*laughs*] But he's in jail, and [*laughs*] I am in an insane asylum and I am a country doctor. I don't know which is worse. But we've remained friends, no less.

INTERVIEWER: How do you get both of these jobs done now?

WILLIAMS: Well [*laughs*] . . .

INTERVIEWER: You publish . . .

WILLIAMS: Yes, yes, I know. But it's, it's a . . . it's like a . . . it's a compulsion, psychologically, like a compulsive drinker. A drinker can always get a drink, you know [*laughs*], even when he shouldn't have it. I've told you enough to show you that writing is so much a part of my satisfaction, part of my personal reaction to life itself, that I write instinctively. I write perhaps to the exclusion of things that a person in my general situation in life ordinarily would do. I don't go out much, I don't play cards, I don't smoke (I did for a while), I drink moderately. Perhaps my poor little wife wishes I would mix more socially with others about us. My inclination is to be, as it has always been, rather by myself. That was one reason for wanting to go into forestry. I wanted to go out among the trees. But Flossie said, "As sure as shooting, you'd find an Indian up one of them, and she wouldn't be a man either!" [*laughs*] But I like to be quiet and think. I'm a pessimist. Not a pessimist in the sense that—look, we won't be alive very much longer, and . . .

INTERVIEWER: Do you really think that?

WILLIAMS: Oh sure. I mean, what is life anyhow? [*sighs*

deeply] Pessimistic optimism [*laughs*]. Um . . . we know nothing.

INTERVIEWER: Well, here you have a poem—

WILLIAMS: Yes sir?

INTERVIEWER: —approximately about that.

WILLIAMS: I think it would do no harm, although I usually object to explaining anything, to mention a few things. By mentioning the baby of course, that puts the poem back thirty-seven years, and today is my . . . baby's birthday,[7] mmmn [*laughs*]. Kathleen was a little girl that we "got," you might say, from the state, the Children's Guardian Association. After all we were poor like most young doctors, and Kathleen came in to help us, so she was the little kid that helped take care of the baby. Well, "Danse Russe." It was the time of our first appreciation of the Russian Imperial School of Dancing when Nijinsky and Pavlova were here. That's the reason, I suppose, that Danse Russe comes in. Anyhow, a dance.

DANSE RUSSE

If when my wife is sleeping
and the baby and Kathleen
are sleeping
and the sun is a flame-white disc
in silken mists
above shining trees,—
if I in my north room
dance naked, grotesquely
before my mirror
waving my shirt round my head
and singing softly to myself:
"I am lonely, lonely.
I was born to be lonely,
I am best so!"
If I admire my arms, my face,
my shoulders, flanks, buttocks
against the yellow drawn shades,—

Who shall say I am not
the happy genius of my household?

INTERVIEWER: I wanted to ask you about that poem, a couple of things. Many many poets have talked about being lonely.

WILLIAMS: Hmmn. Well I think the artist, generally speaking, feels lonely. Perhaps his very recourse to art, in any form, comes from his essential loneliness. He is usually in rebellion against the world, I think. I think that's a rule. I have thought myself that that's rather a snide thing to say—here I am living with my wife and [*laughs*] child and saying, "I'm lonely." It merely records a fact.

INTERVIEWER: Yes, but you, more than most artists, are also living in a community and doing a job in a community.

WILLIAMS: Yes, it's true. But if you do your job, you're sometimes most lonely, strange as it may seem, because in your ordinary work—and there's your incentive for art all the way through—you yourself, as a man, as a woman, as an individual, are very seldom completely involved in your own work, and that answers to some extent the question, "How do you find time for writing?" It's a necessity! Because the essential "I," the person himself, does his work, but remains—after the work is finished, there he stays. Like a man who arrives at the age of sixty-five and retires, or is retired by his firm, and when he gets all through, he finds that he doesn't exist and never has existed, poor guy. He never knew it before. He thought that the job was everything in his life. Well, he's finished. He's absolutely finished! He goes out and shoots himself very often. There is nothing left of him. And I wanted to make very sure that that was *not* going to happen to me, baby, no sir! I knew that if I lived long enough I was going to be old, and after I became old, then life really would begin, as I've said over and over again. Then I would be retired because I've served. I've done my stuff for society, and what's left is my time.

INTERVIEWER: Well, do the people roundabout in Rutherford, your patients and others, know that you're a poet? I mean are they . . .

WILLIAMS: Oh, they're very thoroughly indoctrinated into it now, and the curious thing and one of the most warming things is that they're delighted. They're wonderful about it! Now that during the past four weeks or so, I've had some publicity (which is publicity, just that), oh, they're so thrilled, oh God! "Doc, am I happy! It's wonderful! It's coming to you at last!" As one woman said, "Isn't it great to have all this publicity and get it now while you're alive and not after you're dead?" [*laughs*] Which made me laugh plenty. I thought, Huh, it would be very much better to have it before you're dead, because when you're dead, you're so very very dead! that the publicity would be unimportant, except for your family and probably your heirs, if there are any, or if they get anything out of it.

But a man, an artist, wants a world to be different from what he finds it. So he finds himself lonely. Just the other day, in one of the New York magazines I saw (one of the smaller magazines, I can't recall what its name was . . . *A. P.*, I think, or *A. D.*–oh [*laughs*], *A. P.* is good!–*A. D. 1950*) [*laughs*], there was an article by Cocteau in which he said: The revolution, which every man experiences when he becomes fully aware of life in his own mind, among artists is always at least twenty years before the popular revolution. He sees, inevitably, as an artist or any . . . I won't say any thinking person, but any honestly thinking person (that excludes financiers and economists, those who profit by their careful errors), that anyone who really thinks and knows what goes on in the world, has already been through the revolution in his own spirit, as artists must–they embody it in their technique, and there we come back to my whole reason for being alive.

I believe certain things. I feel that certain things, disastrous things, are happening in the world because of man's stupidity, definite stupidity. I can't do anything about it. Personally, either as a physician or as a citizen, I can do very little but vote, which is a mechanical gesture of some value, of course—I acknowledge it, and I always vote. But in my mind, I've so far gone beyond any of the formal pretexts of politics (whether I'm entirely right or not is another thing) that they seem old hat, most of it. I mean humanly, they are! Every man of any sense knows that the brutality of the world has to be outgrown, that's all. And we outgrow it in our art, in the technique of our art, in the way the line is put down, in the way the colors are applied. I think that the artist really, basically, within himself, is always among the most advanced men of any period. They are the ones who symbolize their thought in their works, and so are always laughed at, inevitably too, because our first reaction is laughter to anything we don't know, laughter or murderous designs. The artist is way ahead of his age in his general thought. And so he's *lonely, lonely*. That's where the loneliness comes from.

INTERVIEWER: Well, if I could bring another man's work into this for a minute.

WILLIAMS: Yes. Yes, do!

INTERVIEWER: I have a poem here by Archibald MacLeish that I came across the other day that is kind of relevant.

WILLIAMS: Yes?

INTERVIEWER: Do you know his "Invocation to the Social Muse?"

WILLIAMS: I just know the name.

INTERVIEWER: Well, he speaks here of this very thing, and then his final question is, "Is it just to demand of us also to bear arms?"—speaking of the poet.

WILLIAMS: Well, there I'd answer the question by saying, we *must* bear arms. In one book of poems called *The Tempers,*[8] I say that the writing of the poem is part of the war. I'm not anxious to rush off and bear arms, but if I should be asked to bear arms, I would do it gladly, and I'd probably be a good soldier, because I know that I am after all one microscopic person, no matter what I may think or no matter whether I believe that I'm doing something valuable or not. And I think a proper citizen of any country or any group should submit himself to the rule of the group in an emergency, though I think there are reasons why we should rebel at times and voice it and go down without a murmur. I don't believe in trying to escape it or lying or cheating or trying to subvert the government by falsity. That I would absolutely oppose in anything! Come out straight, face it and stand up and get it in the face, and say, "Thank you, sir, go ahead and shoot me. I'm much obliged." That's what I think a man is, and I think a poet belongs there.

Now from the other side, it would be valuable for society to pardon Ezra Pound, to bring it right to the point. I think he's much more valuable to society than he is keeping him in an insane asylum. Of course it is a moot point. But I think he is a valuable citizen *as a poet.* He could be guarded, the country could guard itself against him by bringing out what he has to say, letting it be laughed at if necessary, but if it happens to be good, the country should treasure it. I think though that if a draft were necessary to defend the city, whether it's Florence or Geneva or New York or Washington, he should fight right along with the other guys.

INTERVIEWER: How sick do you think Pound is? Do you know?

WILLIAMS: I don't think he's sick at all, I think no more than he has been all his life. He's been an eccentric in the sense that he's off center. Off center, that's what eccentric means. He's been, he's a spoiled brat, and he's carried it into manhood, and he must have his way. I think he's learned a lot by this tragic experience, whether it'll do him any good, whether he'll die before he's released from the mental hospital or not. I think he's always had ideas of grandeur. From the first minute I knew him when he was seventeen, he had to be it. He had to be the big guy. He had to tell everybody. But, nevertheless, I think some of his ideas, some of them, are sound. I am *not* for him in backing Mussolini, though, and we fought it out. He backed Franco, and I took the other side, and we batted it through. For a while I was pretty disgusted with him. I don't follow him politically at all, at all. But I think he's one of our greatest poets, and I wish we could capitalize, since we're a capitalistic country [*laughs*], on his excellences in the art. And he's also a good thinker in economics, but erratic.

INTERVIEWER: I wonder if we could get to your poetry again now, because there're some questions. Let's take just the simple little poem about the plums. Could you read that again?

WILLIAMS: Well, have we got it handy here?

INTERVIEWER: Yes, it's right here.

WILLIAMS: Yeah, all right. Again?

INTERVIEWER: Again, that was just a test that time.

WILLIAMS: Oh, that's right, I forgot that. Can you find it? It's "This Is Just to Say."

INTERVIEWER: I know approximately where it is.

WILLIAMS: That's one thing I would never do, that is, look at an index, that would be acknowledging defeat.

It's curious how a thing of this sort, which was really just a passing gesture, actually took place just as it says here. My wife being out, I left a note for her, just that way, and she replied very beautifully. Unfortunately, I've lost it. I think what she wrote was quite as good as this. A little more complex, but quite as good. Perhaps the virtue of this is its simplicity. Well, let's have it then.

THIS IS JUST TO SAY

I have eaten
the plums
that were in
the icebox

and which
you were probably
saving
for breakfast

Forgive me
they were delicious
so sweet
and so cold

INTERVIEWER: Now what I want to ask you about that, what makes that a poem?

WILLIAMS: In the first place, it's metrically absolutely regular. "This is just to say / I have eaten / the plums / that were in / the icebox / and which / you were probably / saving / for breakfast / Forgive me / they were delicious / so sweet / and so cold." So, dogmatically speaking, it has to be a poem because it goes that way, don't you see!

INTERVIEWER: Well, this goes against so many preconceived ideas of poems [*Williams laughs delightedly*] though, because it's the kind of thing that almost anybody might say.

WILLIAMS: Yes, because no one believes that poetry can exist in his own life. That's one of our immediate fallacies. Some Englishman said, "*Imagine* reading a poem in the American dialects! How impossible!" Well, that's the first hazard, that's the first hurdle, we have to get over that. It has nothing to do with the way it's said. Oh it has something to do, because it can be badly read, and otherwise. But we can't believe that we poor colonials, as we have been ever since the Revolution, we poor people who are not living in the great centers of Europe could have anything happen in our lives important enough to be put down in words and given a *form*. But everything in our lives, if it's sufficiently authentic to our lives and touches us deeply enough with a certain amount of feeling, is capable of being organized into a form which can be a poem. In fact, those simple difficulties, those things which are at the base of all the English departments and all the universities in the world and make them all asinine, because they're usually twenty years back of the times, are the things that make it impossible to *hear* a poem!

We can't even hear it any more because we don't believe it can happen in our lives, our own lives you know, as if we were Greeks who have been dead two thousand years—we're not yet dead, most of us!—some are living on quite dead. But you have to get used to the fact that in your own life, that which touches you, such as your affection for your wife, the woman you happen to be living with (let's not call her wife, that's pure accident), but the woman who's there with whom you are supposed to be in love and sometimes are [*laughs*], if you address something to her, you feel a little sorry—probably the poor kid had these things saved for supper and here you come along and raid it. Why it's practically a rape of the icebox! [*laughs*] And there you are. So I think that's material for a poem [*laughs*], that's really a definite poem without even writing it, but then if you can give it conventional metrical form, why, my God, you're just simply superb, that's all [*laughs*]. You've done a great deed [*laughs*]. That's part of my theory, you see. And it's a unit, it's a unit.

INTERVIEWER: Has your practice mostly been general?

WILLIAMS: I've done a general practice with a strong leaning toward pediatrics. So that I was on the senior staff at the Passaic General Hospital, finally got to be president of the Medical Board and continued there for two or three years (I've forgotten). And then it just coincided with the time that my son came back from the Pacific, his four years. It was fortunate. It was somewhat planned. I mean it was planned to the extent that I did have a son [*laughs*]. That was that. Perhaps if it had been a girl, she'd have been a doctor too, but I thought that sometime in my life, if one of my children turned out to be a physician, that I would "get out" and go into writing, because it was always my idea to go into writing.

It was always important to me to go through the somatic part of medicine into the psychic part, which is verse, which is art, all the way through. I was talking to a man, who teaches at Fairleigh Dickinson, last night, who teaches Modern European History there. He learned that I was a writer and a physician. "Oh!" he said, "that's the real, old humanist school of Europe. All physicians either wrote or painted or at least dabbled a little in one of the arts. And it was the true humanist position." Perhaps I continue it through my parents, who were both born out of the country and who were European minded, my father, although he had nothing immediately English in his makeup, except his blood and his mother (who lived with him or with us), and then my mother whose whole training was French, she studied painting in Paris—perhaps that feeling came over for that reason. And I think to some extent, it's even gone over into my son, for instance, reluctance to charge a poor person more than he can afford to pay. We don't like it. Other fellows don't like it, but they soak them anyhow, but we don't like it, and we don't do it. Not in this house!

That's the reason that I'm in favor of some form of socialized medicine, and I'm on that side. I don't like the person who takes the poor guy and soaks his wife two hundred and fifty dollars for a Caesarean section and then twenty-five dollars for a circumcision, when he hasn't even enough to eat. Now that's the kind of thing that brings medicine into disrepute, and it's done all the time. All the time! Like a woman today even told me she'd been to a local ophthalmologist with her child. She had gone before and was charged three dollars (well, which is modest, for a specialist, but she had nothing), so this time she had been twice with the child, and the fee was "Thirty dollars, thank you," just to look at it and say, "Yes." Well, now you see, a specialist must keep up his place in the world, and he has to compete with the president of the General Motors, and unless the physician can have an income comparable to that of a big businessman, he feels that he's a sucker. And he is, as far as the businessman is concerned, but *not* when he treats the unfortunate person. He doesn't differentiate.

INTERVIEWER: Well, who are most of the people in your practice, for example? I mean do they come from . . .

WILLIAMS: Oh, most of them are commuters. They do

very well, in the five- to twenty-five-thousand-dollar class a year. Oh, they're all right. I have no, well not many, wealthy patients, very few in fact. And I don't any more have the extremely poor, because, frankly, with the money situation what it it, people, generally speaking, have enough, except maybe the teachers in the schools who make very little [*laughs*]. Oh well, two thousand dollars a year isn't much for a young woman. It's fair, but it isn't much. And so forth. But I have a suburban practice among people more or less in my own class, who experience the world very much as others do, [*laughs*] in spite of their veneer and their fear of the *terrible radical*, you know! God, am I a radical!

INTERVIEWER: Oh, are you a radical?

WILLIAMS: I'm a radical! I write modern poetry, baby! [*laughs*] I'm an *awful* person! And I once joined a co-op! My, what a horrible thing that was to most people [*laughs*]. They almost wanted to shoot us. They tried to close the store, forgetting that Boston Common was *commonly* held by the people of Boston, and that was a co-op! Gee, that's the way the country started, you know. But they forget *all that!* "Why, the A & P has to be protected, sir! [*laughs*] This here country [*laughs*], you can't let those *big* people die! Why that's the American way of life! That's the great thing!" So, I don't write conventional poetry, you see. That's the reason for it, because of [*laughs*] that.

INTERVIEWER: Have these people read much of your poetry, do you know?

WILLIAMS: Not if they could help it, they haven't [*laughs*]. But they're good pals. We are good friends. They're some of my best friends. And it's always a good joke, you know.

INTERVIEWER: Find one of your poems there that has a lot of good American in it.

WILLIAMS: Well! Ah yes, let me see, let's take "Ol' Bunk's Band" [*laughs*].

INTERVIEWER: Fine.

WILLIAMS: Ol' Bunk. You see, the theory is, the theory is that you can make a poem out of anything. You don't have to have conventionally poetic material. Anything that is felt, and that is felt deeply or deeply enough or even that gives amusement, is material for art. We don't have to take a conventional subject like Greek drama, which could speak only of the gods, or medieval painting, which was largely devoted to the Christian mythology. We can use anything, anything at all. It's what you *do* with it that counts. It's always been so. It's always been so! Excellence in handling the material is the thing that gives distinction, always. But now we have enlarged the field of choice, that's all. So that if an old colored fellow, who was one of the originators of jazz in New Orleans in 1900, happens to be discovered as Ol' Bunk Johnson was, by a fellow named Williams from Pittsburgh[9] who said, "Gee, I wonder what's happened to Ol' Bunk? I wonder where he is. I wonder if we could find him."

They went down and found him on his little rice farm, and said, "Bunk, do you think you could still play?"

He said, "Yes, I could, if I had my teeth."

"Well," he said, "do you think if we got you some teeth?"

He said, "Yeah, got the ol' horn there, I could try it."

So they got the teeth and gave it to Bunk, and Bunk played all right. So he came up to New York. You didn't happen to be in on it, did you?

INTERVIEWER: I heard it.

WILLIAMS: Wasn't that marvelous though! Well, I was so impressed that I came home and wrote a poem about Ol' Bunk Johnson. This is "Ol' Bunk's Band":

These are men! the gaunt, unfore-
  sold, the vocal,
blatant, Stand up, stand up! the
  slap of a bass-string.

Pick, ping! The horn, the
  hollow horn
long drawn out, a hound deep
  tone–
Choking, choking! while the
  treble reed
races–alone, ripples, screams
  slow to fast–
to second to first! These are men!

Drum, drum, drum, drum, drum
  drum, drum! the
ancient cry, escaping crapulence
  eats through
transcendent–torn, tears, term
  town, tense,
turns and backs off whole, leaps
  up, stomps down,
rips through! These are men
  beneath
whose force the melody limps–
  to
proclaim, proclaims–Run and
  lie down,
in slow measures, to rest and
  not never
need no more! These are men!
  Men!

Ol' Bunk fascinated me! [*laughs*] And there's another one here, if I could find it. Have to be a little cautious, don't we, what we read?

INTERVIEWER: No, we can always cut it out with a pair of scissors.

WILLIAMS: Oh, isn't that good! I was looking for the "Picture of a Nude in a Machine Shop" [*laughs*]. If I could find the gal. She was only on paper anyhow [*laughs*]. Ummn [*searching*], well, maybe it isn't even in here.

INTERVIEWER: I'm not sure it is in this book.

WILLIAMS: I don't think it is, no. Well, one of the old

ones. Let's read one of the older ones, one of the first ones, to show my proclivities as a young man, a very modest young man.

PORTRAIT OF A LADY

Your thighs are appletrees
whose blossoms touch the sky.
Which sky? The sky
where Watteau hung a lady's
slipper. Your knees
are a southern breeze—or
a gust of snow. Agh! what
sort of man was Fragonard?
—as if that answered
anything. Ah, yes—below
the knees, since the tune
drops that way, it is
one of those white summer days,
the tall grass of your ankles
flickers upon the shore—
Which shore?—
the sand clings to my lips—
Which shore?
Agh, petals maybe. How
should I know?
Which shore? Which shore?
I said petals from an appletree.

Wallace Stevens liked this other one, "El Hombre," which is very short. "El Hombre," because I was sick and tired of French titles. You know how the arty person loves to talk French?

INTERVIEWER: Ah, yes.

WILLIAMS: Whether he can talk French or not, he always has to use a French term, that shows that he's smart, I suppose. Well, in order to change that around, I thought Spanish was a good language too, a very much neglected language since Longfellow and, well, who is he anyhow [*laughs*] who wrote "Rip Van Winkle"? Washington Irving! Yes, Irving in his "Alhambra" and Longfellow, they started off in Spanish. We've dropped it in our day, curiously enough, but my parents spoke Spanish, preferably to English, and my brother and I heard it and understood it because they said things in Spanish that they didn't want us to understand. So I liked Spanish [*laughs*], and this is "El Hombre," The Man:

> It's a strange courage
> you bring me ancient star:
>
> Shine alone in the sunrise
> toward which you lend no part! [10]

And then this one. This is hackneyed now, I think. It is to me.

INTERVIEWER: What? "Tract"?

WILLIAMS: You want me to read it anyhow? No?

INTERVIEWER: That's all right, you've recorded that.

WILLIAMS: I've recorded it anyhow. Many things like that have been recorded, and I was glad that Matthiessen left it out of the Oxford anthology of American poems.[11] I think it was a wise thing to do. He did that for others just the same.

INTERVIEWER: Well, what do you think there is about the American language that is so different? You've done more in American than anybody.

WILLIAMS: Well, our lives are lived according to a certain rhythm, whether we know it or not. There is a pace to our lives, which largely governs our lives. There's no question about it. You take a young man who is employed by Standard Oil. Well his life is set to the pace of Standard Oil. He may deny it and think that's a lot of baloney, but it ain't! That's its pace, and the language they speak is his language. I'm not going to fight with him. I'm going to say, that's your language, that's the way you live. It's my job to take it as I find it. I'm no reformer. I take what I find, I make a poem out of it. I make it into a shape which will have a quality which is no longer you. It's come out of you, but I've objectified it. I've given it a form, a human habitation and a place—you know, the Shakespeare stuff.

And it is so. You have to objectify your life, as I've said over and over again. The pianist sits in front of the piano and plays it. He doesn't fall into the strings. He sits there apart and makes a melody of it. So it's up to me. These people are human. I don't fight with them because I don't agree with their ideas. I accept them because they're my friends, because I like their qualities, and because they have an overall quality which is American which they can never recognize unless the artist or the philosopher, but I think largely the artist, presents it as an entity to them, gives them something to believe in, which the artist must do.

We don't know what to believe in. We divide over our religious tenets, unfortunately, unhappily, so that, largely speaking, I never attempt to touch that. I don't attempt to do what Eliot did, go over and take the British religion and make that as his great tenet of life. That's not my business. I'm not that. I'm an artist, if I am anything at all, and so I take the American language as I find it, because in the English language, from which our language is derived, the conventions of speech and the conventions of art, of the poetic line—let's be specific—carry over not only the traditional, which is good (I mean, after all, who can escape the great tradition of the British language?), but they carry over the restricting formulations of that language. They even modify the thought of the language. The forms modify the thought.

That's why the priests of all sorts, the priest, generally speaking, whether Christian or otherwise, sticks to ritual, because he knows if he can get those people to repeat that ritual, they are caught. They are snared, for life, for good or for evil, whatever it may be, but they are snared. And I feel that in a democracy, in a [*sighs*] life that the paleontologists tell us has only existed consciously 700,000 years or something of that sort—a very brief thing—there's a lot yet to discover in the way we behave and what we do and what we think. And the way to discover it is to be an iconoclast, which means to break the icon, to get out from inside that strictly restricting mold or ritual, and get out, not because we want to get out of it, because the secret spirit of that ritual can exist not only in that form, but once that form is broken, the spirit of it comes out and can take again a form which will be more contemporary. So, I think it is our duty as Americans, our devotional duty, let's say, to take out the spirit that has made not only Greek and Latin and French poetry but British poetry also, and which restricts us when we're too stern about following their modes, and put it into something which will be far more liberating to the mind and the spirit of man, if I'm going to be philosophic in that sense. Back of it all, that is the theory. And for that, you have to go into structure, the structure of the line itself.

And you have to build your little model and finally try it out, here and there, and if at the age of sixty-seven, you get a little publicity in *The New York Times Books*,[12] why you're a great man [*laughs*]. You see how important it is [*laughs*]. But the basic thing has nothing to do with that, God help us! Nothing in the world! It's nice to get a prize, it's a little tickling, it's embarrassing, but it's a little bit silly, if I *must* say it [*laughs*], with due respect to my benefactors [*laughs*].

INTERVIEWER: Well, as the man said, though, it's better than after you're dead.

WILLIAMS: [*laughs*] Yeah. Yeah, how do we know? That's a confession of something. Maybe it's much better after we're dead. Who knows? Maybe give us a ticket to the, to the . . . show.

The Editors Meet William Carlos Williams

Dorothy Tooker

William Carlos Williams is, first and foremost, a doctor. That was apparent the day he visited the editors at the *A.D.* office, and that is the unutilized but self-evident key to his literary work. In his letter confirming his appointment with us, he had written that because of previous commitments he had no poetry to offer for publication, but added that he was eager to come, "if it is talk you want so that I can sit back and do nothing more strenuous than spout to my heart's content."

So as soon as we introduced ourselves–Doctor Williams, Tom Ritt, and I–the doctor asked, "What are we going to talk about? And how are you going to use it in *A.D.?*"

I explained that the original prospectus for *A.D.* had included a regular discussion feature between the editors and a prominent writer or other artist. Subject matter was to be broad as the fine arts in general or limited as the writer's pet peeve. This discussion, more than a glorified interview, we envision as a platform for expounding ideas and clarifying concepts which will, insofar as we are able, supplant editorials. "Frequent editorials tend to become either commonplace or supercilious unless there is something really important to be said," Tom Ritt added. "And after all, we *are* striving to make *A.D.* different from the other quarterlies."

Doctor Williams's eyes twinkled as he nodded enthusiastic agreement. "The more new ideas that can be tried out the better."

"That is right in line with something I want to ask,"

Tom Ritt said. "How do you regard obscurity in literature, Doctor? As something necessary or desirable? Or do you believe everyone should be able to understand everything?"

"Somebody's got to know what to hell it's all about," was the emphatic reply. "Not like that painter who was written up in *Life* a while ago. He *tries* to be obscure automatically. No, a writer should not be willfully obscure, but if he has something to say in his own words he cannot wait until the public catches up. And if it doesn't, it's too damned bad."

While he is listening, Doctor Williams regards the speaker with an intensity born of long diagnosing, but as he expounds his own ideas, his eyes focus farther and farther away, as if concentrating on the distant literary horizons toward which his writing has always aimed.

"Yes," he answered after a moment of thought, "A certain amount of obscurity is necessary. You see, so much depends upon the passage of time. The world goes on at its pace and if a man is ahead—well, he stays ahead until the world catches up. It may take years, but that is how we progress.

"Take me with James Joyce. After all this time, I'm still not sure I understand what *Finnegan's Wake* is about. I know it is a dream, and I get the theme of night contrasted with day—and the obscurity of night. But I don't yet know *all* that Joyce meant to convey."

"Why do you use the word 'necessary' in relation to obscurity?" I asked. "Wouldn't 'permissible' be better?"

"No. Obscurity is actually necessary because in making things simple for people you are sacrificing. In talking down, you lose something." Looking over the top of his bifocals, Doctor Williams saw that I was still unconvinced and took a different tack. "Simplicity gets to be dangerous when it is overdone. Look to the artistic standards in Russia. The Soviets have tried to manufacture a vocabulary and presentation understandable to everyone. There is no obscurity there."

I nodded. "Only sterility."

"When a writer has something to say," Doctor Williams went on, looking into a far corner of the room, "it is so important that he can't bother if it is obscure or not. All the ways and means we have of writing just go to prove that no one yet has discovered any one best way. Every creative writer has to experiment, try out new techniques. Someone may catch the element we are all looking for by thrashing around until he blunders into it."

"Certainly in your own work, Doctor, you have never felt confined to traditional forms," Tom said.

"No, I don't believe in it." Doctor Williams straightened up in indignation. "That cussed iambic pentameter! Why, it's done more to stultify poetry in the last few hundred years–gee!" The pause that ensued was more effective in conveying the damage than a dissertation would have been. "When Shakespeare and Marlowe and Ben Jonson sat around the Mermaid Tavern and talked like we are doing, iambic pentameter was wonderfully new and timely. Because they used it superlatively, poets ever since have tried to copy them. The point is not to copy but to imitate –to find forms as suitable for our times as iambic pentameter was for Elizabethan England."

It was easy to remember that this was the man who had once further clarified his ideas by writing: ". . . Shakespeare's 'To hold the mirror up to nature'–as vicious a piece of bad advice as budding artist ever gazed upon. It is tricky, thoughtless, wrong. It is *NOT* to hold the mirror up to nature that the artist performs his work. It is to make, out of the imagination, something not at all a copy of nature, but something quite different, a new thing, unlike anything else in nature, a thing advanced and apart from it. To imitate nature involves the verb to do. To copy is merely to reflect something already there, inertly: Shakespeare's mirror is all that is needed for it. But by imitation we enlarge nature itself, we become nature or we discover in ourselves nature's active part. This is enticing to our minds, it enlarges the concept of art, dignifies it to a place not yet fully realized."

But Doctor Williams was going on. "Forcing twentieth-century America into a sonnet—gosh, how I hate sonnets—is like putting a crab into a square box. You've got to cut his legs off to make him fit. When you get through, you don't have a crab any more."

"My colleague here is gloating over your championing obscurity," I said. "How about a word of caution on the other side? We sit here at *A.D.* day after day reading absolutely un-understandable scripts submitted by kids who worship at the shrine of darkest obscurity. Talk to them, and you find out they look down their noses at you for thinking that anything understandable is not of necessity either decadent or amateurish. This from youngsters who know nothing of the fundamentals of construction, and obviously have no background in literature."

"You're absolutely right. I was talking about great, or at least good, writers with something to say. The preliminaries have to come first, except in the case of genius."

"If only the beginning writers could understand that!" I lamented. "They could save themselves so much heartbreak by a little study. The rest will come. And the sentences they write vertically instead of horizontally, thinking that makes modern poetry—"

"My God, isn't it awful?" he interrupted. "But, of course, we've got to realize that over ninety per cent of what is written as obscure or modern free verse—and there is nothing more stringent and less free in the world than free verse—is sheer hokum."

As I settled back in satisfaction, Tom asked, "Do you think obscurity has any effect upon a writer's writing? I mean, could lack of understanding by the public and critics cripple his writing? Or do you think that is all immaterial to an author with something to communicate?"

"It all depends. A writer's success can definitely be hurt by obscurity if it is judged by popularity or income.

Critics often get down on such a man and hurt his reputation. But if he is a real writer, he will keep on. I never had an audience until I was past fifty. But I wrote all the time anyway. I had to. There were so many things that had to be said!"

Seated with Doctor Williams, that was easily believed. He has a breathless attitude, a quality that is nothing so simple as naiveté. It is a complex wonderment expressed in a long-drawn exclamation of—gosh! Without even stopping to think, one is conscious of the awe with which Doctor Williams must regard the advent of each new life, sensing the potentials of the infant in his hands—an awe something like that of a medical student at his first delivery. But with Doctor Williams there is something further—the understanding and comprehension of a man who has seen more of life and death than the average person. Critics who have described this characteristic of his as childlike have overlooked the insight, the penetration, and cosmic viewpoint from which it stems. It is not a baseless wonder, like that of the young; it is a freshness of viewpoint and outlook arising from clinically minute and meticulous observation coupled with the deep understanding of experienced maturity. When thoughts come too fast for expression or new vistas of unexplored endeavor open in the course of conversation, there is Doctor Williams's characteristic long inhalation followed by a wistfully explosive—gosh! Or at a lesser moment—gee!

"As editors, and writers ourselves, Dorothy and I always like to know an author's reason for writing," Tom said, and Doctor Williams took over again.

"Why write? It's because you are trying to get said what is most important in you. Everyone of us is frustrated. We all want to blossom. Like those desert plants that are all closed and brown until you put them in water. What do you call them?"

"Resurrection plants?"

"That's it—resurrection plants. They unfold and put

out green leaves. We are like that in wanting to expand. We want to communicate the things that are tied up with ourselves.

"When you consider real writing as writing, you must consider that the artist is a rebel. He has to establish his identity artistically and spiritually. He must poke his nose into every corner as far as it will go. He must discover light in obscurity and have the courage to follow his ideals. To stand up for good like bloody hell."

"Then where does censorship come in?" one of us asked.

"The guild of writers belongs to a secret order all its own. There is a type of censorship that will do it no harm, even raise the standards. But if a censor is found to be taking a nonliterary point of view, then that censorship must be destroyed."

"What you were saying a minute ago about an artist following his ideals ties in with both our magazine and another question we wanted to ask," I put in before the conversation turned too far afield. "Just what do you think of the state of writing in America today?"

"Sure it ties in. No man can live without a theory, and we are continually being flooded with new theories and new writers. Some of them are ax grinding, of course, like Hemingway. And that can be bad—bad for both the writer and his art. A good example of that is James T. Farrell. He just keeps on grinding the same old ax, book after book. Nothing changes him. He's not even influenced by his own writing. He doesn't learn nor grow nor expand. It's always the same. His heroines are all alike—she's blonde or brunette—she gets laid or she doesn't. But it's all repetitious."

"But the present trend toward the glorification of perversion in literature seems to be another thing," Tom said. "We have an entire school of writers who find no salvation anywhere—not even within themselves."

There was a worried frown on the doctor's face. "Entirely different. The present trend toward homosexuality in literature is dangerous. It's a tough situation, because it does not necessarily indicate bad writing nor a bad writer. God, I don't know. It's something that has gone on down through the ages, and so far there doesn't seem to be any answer. I'd say that when a work becomes so immersed in it as to spoil literary values, you should omit it. Today it's overdone, too much spread around."

"Don't you feel that America is so permeated with the materialistic that we do not understand anything else?" This from Tom. "There seems to have grown up a cult of introspectively exhibitionistic writing centered about Capote, Vidal, and Tennesee Williams—a whole school of writing. It doesn't seem to me that we have anything to compare with the writing or erudition of some Europeans."

"Such as?"

"Evelyn Waugh in England as well as Elizabeth Bowen and Henry Green. Mauriac, Bernanos, Gide, and Cocteau on the continent. Waugh is a good example. How about his *Helena?* Or did you read *Brideshead Revisited?*"

"Yes."

"Well, what did you think of it?"

"A smart novel by a snobbish person. Why, it wasn't even well written." Doctor Williams spread his broad hands in an apologetic gesture. "Sorry, but that's the way I felt. I know it had some viridical meaning I probably didn't fully get in one reading. But Waugh's snobbish attitude was irritating. And he presented the Catholic Church as too damned smart. I suppose you've got to excuse a certain amount of that in any convert. It's like T. S. Eliot with *his* new church, all spit-licked and polished."

"There's no denying that Waugh is a pronounced British snob," Tom agreed. "But I think you've got to hand it to him in some of his work. *Helena*, for instance. It's a marvelous satire on our times."

"Didn't read it. Seems to me, though, that Eliot is a good takeoff point for what I was saying about Europe. He walked out on America. He tried to become English and take advantage of it. Imagine giving up America—gosh!"

"But where in this country can you find the culture, the generations of refinement, that you can in Europe?" Tom said. "Doesn't a writer need that more than ever in these times?"

Doctor Williams answered eagerly. "Go to Europe by all means. Go to see and learn. But not to imitate. I don't want to sound overly jingoistic, but the fact is that the world force today is here. Here in our own country. We must take advantage of it, work with it, use it."

"Thank goodness *you* said it," I burst out. "I'm so sick and tired of listening to Europe being extolled above and beyond everything. Of course, I believe a writer should have as broad as possible a cultural background. I believe even more than Tom does in a writer knowing the classics of all time, as I said before. But we have something all our own–something vital and alive and new in America. It may not be as polished, but it is rugged and strong."

Our poet was warming to his subject, leaning forward in his chair. "Something new must come out of all this. We must go on originating new forms. Of course there will be lots of blunders, but form is the essential thing. The same old requirements are there to be fulfilled in our own way. If we succeed in that, others will cast their work in the same mold–gee!"

"You sound iconoclastic, Doctor," Tom was leading him on.

"Of course I'm iconoclastic," he came back. "An artist has to be. A continual break down and build up has to go on. Take the forms in which poems are cast. Most of them are old, not suited to our times. We have to cast about searching for new ones, and when we have found them society will finally accept them and see that other work is cast in those forms. Pretty soon, they will become old hat. Somebody else will have to work to get rid of them."

"And you think that is where the future of writing lies–in giving all the experimenters a chance to publish."

"Yes. That's why I'm here today. The whole future of

letters is in youth. That's why literary quarterlies are important, why I always try to help youngsters like you two when I think you have a good thing. Keep that in mind with your editorial work. Try to take a chance on the kids around. Lean over backwards to give them a break. They are the ones who will be doing the writing of the future, and they have to get a start. Keep them going and let them be heard."

We waited without interrupting, for there was obviously more to come, judging by the sheepish smile on Doctor Williams's face. "You might even be the first to publish a real literary figure. Think of it! Like me—I once turned down a poem by a young writer. Turned out his name was Hart Crane!"

Tom whistled as the doctor continued, "Too bad we couldn't have been the first to publish him. But I still think the poem was no damned good!"

When our laughter had quieted down, I said, "I sometimes wonder if we take ourselves too seriously as custodians of good writing and literary progress."

The answer was quick and serious. "Definitely not. *A.D.* and all the other quarterlies have a big job to do. But don't get narrow in your editing. Give every writer your full attention. You have to measure life by elastic standards; otherwise we never can get along together and understand each other. We must draw nearer, not be forced apart."

I thought immediately of the way Doctor Williams had championed our cause in his *Autobiography* just published by Random House. "The little magazine is something I have always fostered; for without it, I myself would have been early silenced. To me it is one magazine, not several. It is a continuous magazine, the only one I know with an absolute freedom of editorial policy and a succession of proprietorships that follows a democratic rule. There is absolutely no dominating policy permitting anyone to dictate anything. When it is in any way successful it is because it fills a need in someone's mind to keep going. When it dies, someone else takes it up in some other part of the country—quite by accident—out of a desire to get the writing down on paper. I have wanted to see established some central or sectional agency which would recognize, and where possible, support little magazines. I was wrong. It must be a person who does it, a person, a fallible person, subject to devotions and accidents."

One thing that impressed me as I sat with Doctor Williams was his quiet faith in the inevitability of progress. Painfully slow though it might be, many false starts as might be made—in the end there will be progression, and it will come through youth. Youth, perhaps with a big helping push from maturity and experience. In spite of Doctor Williams's vitality and enthusiasm he is pervaded with the quietness that comes of assurance. It is like the complete ease of his surgically trained hands that rest motionless, making not the least unnecessary movement, through the most animated conversation.

While I was admiring the controlled discipline of the poet, Tom asked. "Aren't you doing a novel, Doctor?"

"I'm trying, but it's not going very well," he admitted. "It's not fun like poetry. I'm too conscious of form with prose, and the only voluptuous pleasure in writing comes when you can forget yourself. At least that's the way it is with me."

"Tell us about it," Tom urged.

"There isn't much to tell. It's called *The Build-up*, and I'm supposed to have it done by next spring. It is an interpretation of life of about 1905 or '06 after a certain pattern—really very simple. Just the story of an ambitious woman when her family wants to move to the top. I've got about a hundred pages written—and how it stinks! It's terrible!"

He laughed at himself and went on. "You see, I just can't write without getting involved in form. There is no meaning of a novel as a novel. It is the way the thing is written, apart from the story. You should try to modulate your material so as to fit the form in which you are molding it. That's the big thing. And that's where I get all involved."

Doctor Williams gave a prodigious start as he looked at his watch. It was 6:20—we had been talking for over an hour. "I've got to go. I'm late to dinner now!" He smiled ruefully and shook his head. "My wife will be disgusted with me again. Asked me as I was going out what bunch of young damned fools I was off to see this time, and I promised I'd make it home on time tonight. She's used to this, but she thinks I ought to begin to take it easy. She's a good girl, though—gosh!"

There was a world of awe in this last gosh—conveying better than words the patient devotion shown by Mrs. Williams through the busy years—and the unstinting appreciation of the poet who even yet was dazed by his own good fortune in having such a helpmate. As Tom held the doctor's coat, I said, "Bring her along next time. We'd like to meet her, and then she can judge for herself."

"I will," he beamed.

We hope he does.

A Visit with William Carlos Williams

Walter Sutton

WILLIAM CARLOS WILLIAMS has long been a champion of the American idiom as the source of the language and rhythm of modern verse. He speaks here in his own voice in a selection from conversations at his home in Rutherford, New Jersey. Although retired as a physician, Dr. Williams continues the practice of poetry. His latest poems have appeared in *The Hudson Review, Poetry,* and other magazines, and a collection of his plays has recently been published by New Directions. On November 7, 1960, the Poetry Center in New York honored him with a special program given over to a reading of his major poem, *Paterson.*—Walter Sutton

W. S.: One of the things you've mentioned often in writing about modern poetry has been the "variable foot."

W. C. W.: If you want to talk about the variable foot, which is very dear to my heart, I'll begin by saying something about free verse. But, to my mind, there is no such thing as free verse. It's a contradiction in terms. The verse is measured. No measure can be free. We may say Whitman's verse is a typical example of what is spoken of as free verse. Now he himself never called it free verse. It was a term originated I think in France by Paul Fort, who was an innovator, a poet who wrote in the manner of Whitman. And the variable foot is measured. But the spaces between the stresses, the rhythmical units, are variable. Whitman's verse could be counted as spaced, let us say, spaced long or short, but variable.

W. S.: You mean that there are feet, even though the feet may not have regular stresses, as in conventional verse?

W. C. W.: Very definitely, I do.

W. S.: But you wouldn't think of them in terms of stresses?

W. C. W.: No, not as stresses, but as spaces in between the various spaces of the verse. I would say perhaps the confusion comes from my calling them the feet.

W. S.: Your mention of the spacing of the verses reminds me of Charles Olson and his discussion of projective or open verse. Do you think he is following the same line?

W. C. W.: I do, definitely, and it all begins with Whitman, of course. Only Whitman's line is too long for the modern poet. At the present time I have been trying to approach a shorter line which I haven't quite been able to nail. I wanted the shorter line, the sparer line, and yet I want to give a measured line, but the divisions of the line should be shorter.

W. S.: There seems to be a movement in this direction through the three-stepped lines in *Paterson* and the poems in *Desert Music* to the poems that have appeared more recently in the magazines.

W. C. W.: Yes, for my next book, we'll say. Yes, more terse, and absolutely not the stretching out of the line that Whitman did.

W. S.: Now you feel that this change represents an advance for you.

W. C. W.: I very definitely do.

W. S.: That this later work is superior to your earlier verse.

W. C. W.: Yes, the shorter units.

W. S.: Also if we look at a book like Donald Allen's collection of *The New American Poetry*, it seems as though there is a whole younger generation of poets coming along, following the same path.

W. C. W.: Yes, though I maintain that they don't know exactly, metrically, what they're doing, most of them. They have a tendency to call it free verse, but I object.

W. S.: The long line, which you feel is out of joint with the times, you find in Ginsberg and some of the other Beat poets. Do you see a tendency toward more compression in some of the other younger poets?

W. C. W.: Yes, though I've not succeeded in getting them to adopt the term the variable foot. They say what the hell is that, the variable foot?

W. S.: Whether they call it the variable foot or not, many of them seem to be trying to work with verses in the same way. You have mentioned Denise Levertov, and she is very close to you in her way of writing.

W. C. W.: Oh yes, very close. . . . She is from England. But she came to this country to seek a freer relationship to the line in our country, and she has adapted herself completely to our way of listening. She is a very interesting person to me. And she is a very skillful poet. She is half Welsh and half Jewish. That's a curious thing and must have its influence on the writing of her poetry. But she has rebelled from England and come to a freer place. Free construction of the line and has done very well at it.

W. S.: She is often named with the Beats, isn't she?

W. C. W.: Yes, she was in San Francisco. She's in New York now. And she is definitely classed among the modern American poets. Classed as what we'll call a Beat, we'll say. Too bad to know them as Beats. But the Beats haven't contributed anything much. I encountered the work of Kerouac. I was tremendously disappointed. Awful. It's a prose work. But for God's sake, what he is attempting to do, I just don't know. Well, I think Denise has a sense of metrical arrangement of lines which is not the conventional thing, but it has a unity. . . . I feel closer to her than to any of the modern poets. She is more alert–very much more alert to my feeling about words–As Flossie says, she is America's woman poet of the future.

W. S.: Most of the younger poets in Allen's collection acknowledge the influence of both you and Pound.

W. C. W.: Gee, Pound is– I've written a letter to Pound saying that he is the first who has used in his writing as a poet the American idiom. But he has not answered me. Doesn't dare, I think.

W. S.: You probably insulted him.

W. C. W.: Yes, I think so. I hope so. But it came as a flash of insight into his poetry. Into the poems he has written, which are never regular, never strictly measured. . . .

W. S.: But the younger poets, including Olson, seem very much aware of what you and Pound have done. Wouldn't you say that Olson's poem on Gloucester is close to your work, as well as to Pound's?

W. C. W.: Oh yes, Flossie has read the whole of Olson's Maximus poems to me. The earlier Maximus poem has been very much modified in the final printing and is not the same poem at all. I don't know whether I like it as much as I did, but it is very much more closely identified with Gloucester, the sea people, and the sailors. . . . He must have shifted in his own mind what he was going to say. He must have realized that it was a sea poem. Very definitely more so than he first intended. . . . And how he wrote the poem down on the page was very interesting to me. And the shorter lines. Anti-Whitman. It's a good example of what has happened to Whitman. Olson's line is very much more in the American idiom. A shorter division of the lines, not the tendency of Ginsberg. He went back. His longer lines don't seem to fit in with the modern tendency at all. Retrograde. I didn't like them at all in *Howl!* If he had paid attention to what Olson was doing it would have been more successful. . . . Olson does identify himself with Gloucester and the sailors, and it might have been a better poem if it had been more so. Maybe not calling it Maximus, but calling it Gloucester. It would be more understandable. But he wants to call it Maximus. And what is the definition of Maximus? I'd like to hear him talk about that. What does he mean by Maximus? Maximus means the furthest development of something.

W. S.: I suppose this could be the extension of personality. To encompass the world. As in Whitman's idea of embracing, of speaking for more than himself—

W. C. W.: I'd like to hear him talk about it. What Maximum has to do with Gloucester. Gloucester is a very circumscribed image. But it is an attractive image to me. Very. It is an American image, developed in America, in an environment with which he was familiar as a child. And it developed his conception of his childhood. Maybe a maximum conception. That would make it much more important to me. And he is not English in any sense, but writes in the American idiom developed to the maximum proportions. . . .

W. S.: You have mentioned Whitman several times. Wasn't he one of your early favorites?

W. C. W.: Whitman was the first American poet that I was interested in. I was reading him in 1903 when I first went to Penn. My wife had presented me with the *Leaves of Grass* before we were married, and I took that book with me, and I absorbed it with enthusiasm. I loved to read the poems to myself. I don't know why I had that instinctive drive to get in touch with Whitman, but he was a passionate man, and the first great poem, "The Song of Myself," was more or less an adolescent poem, I think, because it was throwing away any hold the classics had on him. He didn't know where to go, perhaps, but he didn't know anything about the English language as taught in England, and he wanted to be himself, and he couldn't contain himself any longer. So he just leapt off, and he was driven to find a way for himself, like the American pioneers, we'll say. He had to go. He didn't know where to go, and he wrote the way he felt. And it was not studied because he didn't know how to study it.

W. S.: Do you think that his desire to provide a scripture of some kind might have been the reason for his shifting to something closer to a Biblical form than to the form of conventional English verse?

W. C. W.: I don't hear any Biblical form in his poems.

W. S.: I was thinking of his using parallelism to form verses rather than following the conventional way.

W. C. W.: It may have been the Bible that started him off, but he persisted in going astray, and he would not be disciplined. Aside from the discipline of his own voice.

He must have said them aloud. I never thought of that. But he must have recited what he had to say aloud. To neighbors, we'll say, and friends. I don't know whether it's recorded that he did recite or not. . . .

W. S.: You have also said that you think of Pound as standing at the beginning of modern American verse. How do you see his contribution as being different from that of Whitman?

W. C. W.: But Pound was *disciplined*. He was a scholar, no matter how faulty a scholar. He was following the scholarship of Europe. And the songs of Europe. The Provençal. He was a student of English and Provençal and French, and, to a certain extent, Spanish. But he didn't acknowledge Whitman as a master.

W. S.: He does have a poem that says that he had had a quarrel with Whitman but that it's time to make up. You broke the wood, he said, and it's time for us to do the carving.

W. C. W.: Yes, it is a poem that was inspired by Whitman's example. But both Eliot and Pound rejected Whitman as a master. He didn't have anything to teach them. But they didn't *know* what he had to teach them. The idiom itself, which they did not acknowledge.

W. S.: Although Pound sometimes uses an exaggerated American dialect.

W. C. W.: He tends to clown it as Lowell does, in a Yankee farm accent, but he doesn't do it well. He clowns it so obviously that– It's a kind of hayseed accent, which is entirely in his own mind. No one would ever talk that way.

W. S.: Is this the voice you hear in the letters often?

W. C. W.: Why, I think so. . . . He thinks he's smart, and he's not smart. He's inaccurate. He attempts to make fun of all American speakers, but he doesn't know what he's talking about.

W. S.: This is the role he puts himself into as Old Ez–

W. C. W.: Agh, Old Ez. A pain in the ass.

W. S.: Does he talk that way too?

W. C. W:. Yes, he does, once in a while. I think it was

personally directed toward making fun of me, as an American.

W. S.: Trying to talk to you in your own language–

W. C. W.: Why yes, that's the thing, more or less, and it didn't go over with me. He doesn't know how I talk or how an American talks. The way an American talks is unimportant to him, so that he's liberated to make fun of it. But there's something else which he doesn't know. . . . I've been insisting that since the day of Pound a cultured American language, which was different from English, which was not recognized by Pound, has grown up. And that particularly in our poetry made an idiom of its own in the early years of the twentieth century. It had not been recognized as a poetic language at all, and all our generation was rejected, because we didn't speak *English*, the English of the schools. But we were–I was talking a language I was familiar with, that I got from–Polish people, we'll say, any man that would talk to me at all. Pound would want to take it to Harvard, or some such place.

W. S.: You think that there is a native cultural language, which is cosmopolitan, as well as the foreign cultured languages that Pound was interested in?

W. C. W.: Yes, and Pound has not been completely frank with me. He wants me to be known as a more or less uneducated man. And I–as far as I'm concerned–I knew a damn sight more French than he did. I was not completely read in English or American literature, but I was gradually setting up another fund of knowledge of poems. . . .

W. S.: As for Eliot, I think that at one time, or more than one time, you referred to *The Waste Land* as a kind of disaster for modern verse.

W. C. W.: Yes, I read it with a great deal of interest. And Pound had read it before it was published as Eliot's work. The secret of Pound's admiration for this poem of Eliot's, which Pound had worked on–it impressed him. Here was a cultured man, much as he was. And the only difference between Pound and Eliot was that Pound wasn't impressed in the same way. He didn't want to be English.

And Eliot wanted to. Something happened in his soul, we'll say (I don't want to use the word *soul*), but something happened to his Christian soul that convinced Eliot that he was going wrong. And therefore he had to correct himself. In a very well-known appearance at Columbia University he acknowledged the whole thing. He adopted the Church of England and all the Christian dogmas of his church. . . . And he followed Milton. And I was particularly offended because in my reading of Milton, I found him to be using inversions of phrase which offended me, because I couldn't speak my own language without using, freely, inversions, which Shakespeare also does. But I wanted to get rid of using inversions of phrase—Latinizations—and so, taking a backdoor approach, I was forced to consider a variation of the phrase in the manner of Whitman. If I'm going to use my language, my own language, I had to have the dignity, the effrontery, to follow a new pattern. But Eliot wouldn't do that. He would give up his language and go to a type of religious experience that would permit him to talk in a British manner, even if it had to be known that it was also the manner of Shakespeare. But to talk in the American idiom you can't talk as Shakespeare used to talk, or Milton, or Eliot. You have finally to get away from this pattern of speech and invent another speech . . . to be formed, to be patterned after a new mode. I've got myself in wrong before the critics by attempting to bring in the idea of mathematics. Of Einstein. Not Einstein, we'll say, but Einstein's ideas. The uncertainty of space.

W. S.: Or of time, as something that can no longer be measured in the same way. You have suggested that this is something that affects a poet regardless of whether he is familiar with the theory in a technical way. That he is simply living in a world that is somehow different—

W. C. W.: Yes, a very different world. And maybe it's impossible to write poetry conventionally. I think it is. But there is another way of doing it, and this—without knowing it—Whitman stumbled on. . . . But there is the practical problem of the writing of a modern poem, an American poem, on the page, which anyone who faces it has to acknowledge as very complicated, and very difficult. And it begins in the adoption of the American idiom. If you write poems in that way you have to do certain things with the poem. To make it good. To make it subtle. To make it responsive to strange pressures. And many poets don't do it, and most of them write very tiresome verses, metrically.

W. S.: Could you say something about these things that happen to the language. Or is this untranslatable?

W. C. W.: It's untranslatable but it's not English. . . .

W. S.: When you said something about the way the poem goes down on the page, I was reminded of a Cummings poem.

W. C. W.: Yes, Cummings has very much to say, and he speaks in the American idiom. I think that if Cummings was asked to write a typically British poem governed by the English academy, he would have great difficulty. But not entirely, because after all Cummings is an English scholar—

W. S.: And he loves the sonnet.

W. C. W.: Yes, he does love the sonnet. But he is very conventional when he writes his little lyrics in *da ding da ding da ding da ding*. He is not convincing to me. He's not subtle at all.

W. S.: Do you think there is a difference in quality between his conventionally rimed poems and his relatively free poems?

W. C. W.: These relatively free poems are when he does his best work. He *stretches* a bit. To make something come into the pattern. But he has never named the thing that he does, which I have attempted to name. And maybe come a cropper. When Cummings does a conventional poem, he speaks a really vulgar language, anything he wants to say, but he's not satisfactory. Sometimes he's just prosy. . . .

W. S.: Keats he liked especially, who was also one of your favorites—

W. C. W.: Oh, yes, my first poet that I recognized was Keats. I didn't know anything at all about language, and I was a medical student, but I got great emotional satisfaction from hearing Keats read–*Hyperion,* I believe.

W. S.: Was it the sensuousness?

W. C. W.: I don't know what it was. I was writing a long poem. Wasn't counting at all, just putting it down, presumably blank verse. I thought I was writing blank verse, but thank God it's all been destroyed. It was a very romantic poem. I was writing that when I was an intern at French Hospital in New York, and I was to write this long poem which was terrifically romantic. God knows where that came from.

W. S.: This was before you made the break from conventional verse.

W. C. W.: Yes, before I even knew Pound. I had to do something. I was determined that it would be a poem. I didn't know what a poem should be–what it should be like.

W. S.: But you were finding out–

W. C. W.: I was finding out, more or less. But, well, from that time I went along with Pound. Later on, he switched to Eliot and his *Waste Land,* which I admired too, but I was intensely jealous of this man, who was much more cultured than I was, and I didn't know anything about English literature at all. But when I recognized what he was doing I didn't like it at all. He was giving up America. And maybe my attachment to my father, who was English and who had never become an American citizen influenced me because I was– You know, the Oedipus complex, between father and son–I resented him being English and not being American. And that was when Eliot was living in England and had given up America.

W. S.: I see that you have been reading Shapiro's *In Defense of Ignorance.* What do you think of his describing Pound and Eliot as intellectuals and culture poets, while you are seen differently, as a kind of primitive–

W. C. W.: Not primitive. Inventive. But I find something in the body of the poetry which is very difficult to approach. Very difficult to make a construction that will be new. I think occasionally I get a tremendous thrill when I have written something. I say *Jesus*, that's *new!* That's nothing that anyone else is doing, and I have great difficulty to pull off a little patch of life in the language I know, which is the American idiom, which the English can't duplicate, because they're not inventing any more. All has been done for them. But they can repeat a language. A beautiful language. But not invent in it. The construction can't be invented by them. And in my language I can find some release with a hard effort, which is invention, hard effort when I want to say something, to speak in some way, to construct a poem that will not be a sonnet and not be a quatrain at all but very sensuous and that wanders over the page in a very curious way that has never before been encountered. The poem is here but the metric is here, and they go along side by side—the verbal invention and the purely metrical invention—go along arm in arm, looking for a place that they can embrace, we'll say, and then they go together. Why, they strike it off. And that's a *poem!* That's very seldom found, and we have the same thing in any poet.

W. S.: The marriage of language and metric?

W. C. W.: Yes, and you can fight and fight and fight a lifetime till you hit a fusion.

W. S.: And you feel this is easier to do in the American idiom than in British English?

W. C. W.: Yes, the English are not inventive any more. Englishmen and Englishwomen are not dead, we'll say, but—

W. S.: Poetically dead, you'd say?

W. C. W.: I think they are poetically dead.

W. S.: Did you also mean that the English poets may be imitating themselves, or their past?

W. C. W.: Yes, I think they are.

W. S.: Do you see any departures from this at all?

W. C. W.: They try their best, but they just go over and over and over.

W. S.: It is rare for an English poet to break away from regular meters.

W. C. W.: Well, what can they do? They're cultured

gentlemen, and we know what that thing means. They're goddam liars.

W. S.: You don't think that poetry is compatible with the cult of the gentleman?

W. C. W.: No, the cult of the gentleman will lead him to double-cross a man. The really cultured gentleman will do you dirt if he can get away with it, and not be found out.

W. S.: Of course, there are some of the younger English writers who are reacting against the old order, or the Establishment, as they call it, men who are in a way really antigentlemanly. This may be more apparent in the prose than in the poetry. Do you notice any evidence of this attitude in the poetry?

W. C. W.: No, I haven't. Though there is a young English poet I have not met, who has not been outside of England. Out of Cambridge, we'll say. Who is translating Catullus. It is supposed to be one of the best, the most undisciplined bawdy translations. He has been rejected by the British scholars at the present moment. And I'm going to hear more about him. He is the most delightful translator of Catullus.

W. S.: Have you seen some of it in manuscript, or has some of it been published?

W. C. W.: I have some here. A few of the poems were published in *Agenda* [London]. Peter Whigham is his name. Well, he's writing now, and he's trying to get a publisher. He's working on it. He's young. It'll be a wonderful thing, to have Flossie read it to me. . . .

W. S.: Another thing I wanted to ask you about is the status of the poet. When Pound first went abroad, there was a sense of the alienation of the poet. He wrote poems about the artist being cast away in the American village, lost in a Philistine culture. And in some of your poems you wrote about the fact that your townspeople were not aware that there was a poet living among them who might be important to them, even though he wasn't recognized. What kind of change in the status of the poet do you see over the past fifty years?

W. C. W.: Oh, very much improved. Partly by the women, we'll say, by the attempt of the women to recognize poetry and art of all kinds. It has made the men conscious that they are missing something. When I first attempted to read poetry thirty-five or forty years ago, at church functions, or club functions, they always wanted to hear me say something shocking. Now, I wanted to shock them by reading some of the shocking poems I had attempted to write—and I did write—and they would burst into raucous cheers when I would say anything shocking, and that was being a poet, to be careless of what other people say. And that was taken up by the Beatniks. They attempt to show they don't care about the conventions by using vulgar words and cursing—They want to appear tough.

W. S.: But this battle is largely in the past, except for the Beatniks?

W. C. W.: Yes, the reception of poetry by the general public is very much better than it used to be. It used to be that when I attempted to read poetry they could not understand what I was talking about in the first place. And any man who dealt with poetry must be effeminate. And therefore he must compensate. But that's entirely in the past. I'm accepted by the ordinary people I know, my friends, in my town. They have come to accept me.

W. S.: You feel that there is a respect that had been lacking?

W. C. W.: Yes, a very great respect. I'm accepted, and admired, and envied, to a certain extent. As I've gotten older, I've been more accepted by the general public. I've been praised, more than I want to be. They don't understand what the hell I'm driving at, but they accept me.

W. S.: And beyond the community the modern poet has an increasingly wide reading audience. The fact that colleges include modern poetry in their curriculums has helped.

W. C. W.: Even high schools. I've been asked to read, and I've been appreciated. I've had many letters from high-school kids, both male and female. . . .

W. S.: The attitude of society toward the poet has changed. What about the poet's attitude toward society? You once wrote an essay called "Against the Weather," the idea being that the artist or poet has to be in resistance to the currents of his time. Is that still your opinion?

W. C. W.: Yes, it's still my opinion. Definitely.

W. S.: In *Paterson* there is a criticism of the society expressed. And some of the ideas in the poem suggest a sympathy with the ideas of Pound even though you may not agree with him politically.

W. C. W.: Yes, though I don't know specifically what you're aiming at.

W. S.: I was thinking of the section on money, for example.

W. C. W.: Oh, yes, I was very sympathetic with Pound, in this way. For my father was always interested in socialism. And he used to have books around the house, which I didn't bother to read very much, but he was really a socialist to a certain extent. He would have been a socialist if he had lived in England at this time. And I always had a sympathetic feeling toward socialism, and when Pound began to talk about it, he interested me in Major Douglas. I tried to read up on Major Douglas's work. . . .

W. S.: Pound went back into the bank war in the *Cantos*—

W. C. W.: Oh, yes, I'm out of sympathy with all our capitalists to this day. Money is the death of America. And it's coming out more and more in our present difficulties with Russia.

W. S.: Do you think that this is something that a poet is usually sensitive to?

W. C. W.: I think so. He can't be a poet without knowing about interest and money. It's not human to ignore the people.

W. S.: You made some reference to socialized medicine. I gather that this is something you were in favor of as a physician.

W. C. W.: Yes, I've always been fighting with the organization of the doctors. And organized medicine. They are the type of men as doctors which I particularly despise. Doctors who practice medicine for money and not for humanity. I know too many men who have just wanted to keep the price of medicine up so that they get their divvy. My idea of the old doctor is not the money-grabbing type, who has to make money to get on. It's not sympathetic to me.

W. S.: The fourth book of *Paterson* suggests also that both as a doctor and as a poet you were thinking of the word cancer in both a medical and an economic sense.

W. C. W.: Well, money is a cancer.

W. S.: Of course, in Pound, the usura theme is strong all through the *Cantos*. Do you think this is a point of contact between your work and his?

W. C. W.: I was very conscious of it, all during those years, and I identified myself with him as far as I was able to, to assist him. But he had some crazy ideas, which made me laugh. He always had to pretend to know more about medicine than I did. . . .

W. S.: Many of your poems have references to painting.

W. C. W.: Yes, because of my interest in painting, the Imagists appealed to me. It was an image that I was seeking, and when Pound came along with his drive for the image it appealed to me very strongly. Poetry and the image were linked in my mind. And it was very natural for me to speak of poetry as an image and to write down a poem as an image and to leave it to the natural intelligence of a man. . . . If an image were set down on canvas, it was both a poem and a picture at the same time, and it was a very fertile thing to me to deal with. . . . When I found Pound talking of the image I accepted it as a poem. . . . I've always admired painters; my best friends have been painters. Charles Demuth is one of my earliest friends, and when I went to Philadelphia to study medicine, I ate in the same boardinghouse that he did. . . . The image of a painting identified the man as a poet to me.

W. S.: And you never found it difficult to communicate

with painters? Somehow you feel that you and they speak the same language?

W. C. W.: Yes, very close. . . . And as I've grown older, I've attempted to fuse the poetry and painting to make it the same thing—

W. S.: Is one of the things you do to abstract the elements of the work or the images from the work, or whatever the forms may be, in a way that indicates what seems to you to be somehow the essential principle of design involved?

W. C. W.: Very definitely, very well stated. The design of the painting and of the poem I've attempted to fuse. To make it the same thing. And sometimes when I write I don't want to say anything. I just want to present it. Not a didactic meaning. I don't care about the didactic meaning —the moral. To add some tag is absolutely repulsive to me.

W. S.: You're interested in it as an abstract work regardless of whether it's representational or not?

W. C. W.: Yes, I don't care whether it's representational or not. But to give a design. A design in the poem and a design in the picture should make them more or less the same thing.

W. S.: Is painting closer to you than music?

W. C. W.: Yes, to me it's closer than music. Music doesn't mean much to me. I like old-fashioned music, I think, but I'm not very sympathetic to this modern atonality. Painting is much more my meat. Maybe, we'll say, the Renaissance, the big murals at the Vatican—they make much more sense to me. Also, I was tremendously involved in an appreciation of Cezanne. He was a designer. He put it down on the canvas so that there would be a meaning without saying anything at all. Just the relation of the parts to themselves. In considering a poem, I don't care whether it's finished or not; if it's put down with a good relation to the parts, it becomes a poem. And the meaning of the poem can be grasped by attention to the design.

W. S.: One of the artists you mention in *Paterson Five*

is Toulouse-Lautrec. Is he interesting to you because he is the artist of the whorehouse, as you call him, or because of the nature of his work?

W. C. W.: Well, I was attracted to Toulouse-Lautrec by his social position, which I sympathized with. A whore is just as much a human being as a saint, and I wanted to emphasize that. He is a man that respected the truth of the design. For God's sake, what the hell difference is it to him that she's a whore? He was indifferent to it, and the poet is also indifferent to it. . . .

W. S.: There is a kind of identification here of the painter with the outcast, which is, I suppose, partly a rebellion, or a gesture.

W. C. W.: It is very definitely a gesture. Villon was a reprobate, but he was a truth-speaker. Truth in the sense of the artist. And the artist can't bother about what people are thinking.

W. S.: Do you think that part of the appeal of the prostitute as a subject is that the prostitute doesn't have to be conventional in the way that a lady is?

W. C. W.: Yes, she's a professional figure as a model. All artists are moved by real human relations and not artificial, which all the rest of us need to respect. If the ordinary people have to be divided by social relationships, the artist has to get away from that to real human truth.

W. S.: By breaking through restricting conventions?

W. C. W.: Yeah, well—children don't respect social distinctions if they have any chance to determine their own position in the world, until they have been perverted by their elders and forced into certain categories, for instance, Catholic, Protestant. Ph-h-h, for God's sake, what is that to an artist? It's worse than idle to think about. Villon was a Catholic, and he respected the forms because he was damn well made to do it. . . .

W. S.: You said you don't like much modern music. What is your feeling about jazz, and the attention that the Beat poets have given it?

W. C. W.: The Beat generation has nothing to do with beat, and they should if they're interested in jazz because jazz is always percussive. But in jazz music even the saxophone sounds are not advanced enough from the primitive to interest me at all. I don't like jazz. The artists in Paris rave about jazz, but it's too tiresome, it's too much the same thing.

W. S.: There's not enough variability?

W. C. W.: Not variability at all. Not subtle. And if you've got to be sexually excited by it, it shows you to be a boob. It merely excites; there's no subtlety at all. . . .

W. S.: From what you have said about jazz, and other things as well, it seems that the critics who have tried to classify you as a primitive may be off the beam.

W. C. W.: I think so. I was very sexually successful, as a young man, but I did not believe in going so far that I lost my head. I wanted always to be conscious. I didn't want to indulge in sex so much that I lost my head.

W. S.: This may be a distinction to make between you and the Beats, since I think that in Beat poetry there is often the desire to get beyond consciousness somehow–

W. C. W.: Yes, I think so very definitely.

W. S.: –through jazz or sex or dope, or whatever it may be.

W. C. W.: Dope! That I have no sympathy for at all! I want to be always deeper intellectually– That's a bad term to use–*intellectually*–because it makes you think of the thinker, but I don't think that the thinker's thinking anything out any more than Kant thought out in his *Critique of Pure Reason.* What did he think he was coming to? Except futility. And I don't believe in the Beat. I've known some of the Beat poets. But they only confuse themselves. That is, an anti-Beat tenet of mine would be the variable foot. But what do they know about the variable foot? They've never thought anything about it. They don't even know that poetry is written in measurable feet.

W. S.: Is that one reason why this poetry can be read

with jazz? Because it doesn't have a beat of its own anyway, would you say?

W. C. W.: That is a very good thought. I think it is because they want to be *primitive*. And they *want* to be primitive.

W. S.: Self-consciously.

W. C. W.: Yes, self-consciously. And they can't be primitive. The only thing they can be is more thoughtful than ever. . . . I've known many primitive people, but they are surprisingly complex when you get to know them. Their primitive natures disappear. They become quiet. We value them as individuals not because of their beat characteristics but because they are capable of becoming more like us.

W. S.: As for the Beats, you have been associated with a number of them, as you have with younger poets generally, and I think that at least in the beginning of the movement there might have been the idea that you were—

W. C. W.: One of them? And then that's where we parted company. I can't believe you can excite yourself, brainlessly, into being a member of the Beat generation. I think that a poet should be understanding.

W. S.: You don't feel then that to any extent you have been a father of the Beat generation.

W. C. W.: No. No. It has been accidental that I knew Allen Ginsberg. My only association with him was that he had something to say and I wanted him to say it. And I wanted to befriend him. But I am not thoroughly satisfied with what he has done. I have told him—I mean I am disgusted with him and his long lines.

W. S.: Don't you think that this movement seems to be receding anyway, by now?

W. C. W.: Receding because of their inability to make themselves think. And they tend toward homosexuality. For God's sake, what's homosexuality? A variant of sexuality. The same thing. There's nothing new about that. It's been done before. And no *enlightenment* . . . .

II
Dialogues

Excerpts from a dozen other interviews with Williams are arranged by subject matter to follow. The source of each quotation is listed in parentheses at the close of the excerpt, according to this key.

AS: Williams's "Faiths for a Complex World," *American Scholar,* XXVI, Fall, 1957, pp. 453-57.

B: "Talk with William Carlos Williams by Harvey Breit," *The New York Times Book Review,* XV, 3 (Sunday, January 15, 1950), 18. Reprinted in *The Writer Observed,* Cleveland, The World Publishing Co., 1956, pp. 99-101.

GG: The Golden Goose, "Symposium on Writing," Series 3, No. 2, Autumn, 1951, pp. 89-96. Williams's remarks are taken from wire recordings made in August of 1950 by R. W. Emerson for Station WOSU in Columbus, Ohio, broadcast Oct. 7, 1950 on the weekly poetry program "Voices."

GG,U: The Golden Goose, "Note on University Instruction in the Nature of the Poem," No. 3, June, 1949, pp. 29-30.

IW: I Wanted to Write a Poem, Williams's informal bibliography, with Edith Heal, Boston, The Beacon Press, 1958.

ND 17: "Appendix IV," a conversation between Williams and John C. Thirlwall, 307-10, appended to Thirlwall's essay, "William Carlos Williams's *Paterson*" in *New Directions 17* (1961), pp. 252-310.

PR: "William Carlos Williams," an interview by Stanley Koehler taped in April of 1962, published in *Paris Review,* VIII, No. 32, Summer-Fall, 1964, pp. 110-51.

Part R: "The Situation in American Writing," *Partisan Review,* IV, No. 4, Summer, 1939, pp. 41-44. Answers to a questionnaire sent to such writers as John Dos Passos, Gertrude Stein, John Peale Bishop, Sherwood Anderson, Robert Penn Warren, and others, in addition to Williams.

PMC: "Poet-Pediatrician Tells Why He Chose to Write about Paterson," *Paterson Morning Call,* Paterson, New Jersey, May 4, 1950, p. 12.

T: Transcriptions by John C. Thirlwall of his conversations with Williams from 1953 to 1960. See also *ND 17.*

MW: "Mike Wallace Asks William Carlos Williams: Is Poetry a Dead Duck?" *The New York Post,* Oct. 18, 1957, p. 46. (First half of interview included in *Paterson V,* New Directions, pp. 261-62.)

We: Mike Weaver's quoting of an early (1913?) Williams's essay, "Speech Rhythm," located among the Viola Baxter Jordan papers at Yale, pp. 82-83 of Weaver's *William Carlos Williams, The American Background,* Cambridge, The University Press, 1971.

On the American Idiom

WILLIAMS: We were speaking straight ahead about what concerned us, and if I could have overheard what I was saying then, that would have given me a hint of how to phrase myself, to say what I had to say. Not after the establishment, but speaking straight ahead. I would gladly have traded what I have tried to say, for what came off my tongue, naturally. . . .

INTERVIEWER: Was this in line with what the others in the group were trying to do?

WILLIAMS: I don't think they knew what they were trying to do; but in effect it was. I couldn't speak like the academy. It had to be modified by the conversation about me. As Marianne Moore used to say, a language dogs and cats could understand. So I think she agrees with me fundamentally. Not the speech of English country people, which would have something artificial about it; not that, but language modified by *our* environment; the American environment. (*PR*, pp. 9–10)

This seemed to me to be what a poem was for, to speak for us in a language we can understand. . . . We must know it as our own, we must be satisfied that it speaks for us. And yet it must remain a language like all languages, a symbol of communication. (*ND 17*, p. 254)

Obviously the first thing to do is to establish a department of the American language: a Chair, that is, of our language which would have primacy over the teachings of all other languages at the university. Under this would come other languages bearing on our own: German, French, Spanish, Portuguese, and of course, English.

Second, we should have to differentiate a modern prosody or method of construction of the poem from the conventional English and French modes which are standard for those languages. We should have to insist that English prosody as established by English custom . . . is a purely arbitrary matter wholly unrelated to our own language or necessity.

This is most important, for until we disabuse ourselves of the notion that English prosody is an inevitable and God-given rule for us as for the English, we shall remain impotent.

Next we must establish in our minds the historical fact that the American Language invaded both English and French in the nineteenth century. . . .

The invasion, the modification of Yeats' corpus by the direct criticisms of Ezra Pound, Joyce (who never failed to read his Paris edition of the *Herald-Tribune* lest he miss the sayings of Andy Gump), Gertrude Stein, Hemingway, etc., etc. The thing to bear in mind is that it is the American language penetrating the European literary modes which should be studied. (*GG, U*)

Poetry is in a chaotic stage. We have to reject the standard forms of English verse and put ourselves into chaos on purpose, in order to rediscover new constellations of the elements of verse in our time. We have to break down poetry into its elements just as the chemists and physicists are doing. In order to realize ourselves. In order to reform the elements. (*B*)

On the Anti-poetic

The commonest situations in the world have the very essence of poetry if looked at correctly. If I take a dirty old woman in the street, it is not necessary to put her in the situation of a princess. All poets have a tendency to dress up an ordinary person, as Yeats does. It has to be a special treatment to be poetic, and I don't acknowledge this at all. I'd rather look at an old woman paring her nails as the essence of the "anti-poetic." . . . I think that what Stevens said [1] was nonsense. I wanted to get to the real situation, not human nor aesthetic—almost a philosophic truth which can ignore all human categories. (*T*)

On Art

The arts, music and painting, or the plastic arts, are important to a man by way of relief from his main task. . . . The mind can't work to the full of its bent unless he has this relief. One morning, after a relaxing sleep, he wakes, perhaps in the dark before dawn, and what has been lacking in the technique of the ingredient of a stain appears in a flash, and the details fall open to his eyes. . . .

These are princely dreams. Pasteur once said that a man cannot go on without a theory to guide him. The thing that sustains a man among his fellows is his secret opinion of himself. On the instant I look into a man's eyes I know what that man amounts to for me and know how to deal with him. . . . A big dollar sign shows me at once to beware.

If a man is of the royal blood, an artist—and it is the life of an artist which I have been attempting to indicate here—he will be above all this. He can't afford to be caught at it. That is why men with whom you want to be associated keep themselves mostly silent, frequent mostly the family circle and groups of intimates. They do not give themselves away; the best of them are enigmas to their fellows, covertly open in their dealings with other men. They have nothing to sell. (*AS*, pp. 455–56)

I think the young man is likely to be carried away by

his passion; but the old man, if he is wise, knows *why* he is writing a good poem. I like to think of the Japanese print maker Hokusai who said that (he lived to be ninety-nine) when he arrived at age a hundred, every dot on his paper would be significant. If your interest is in theory, as Pasteur's interest was in theory, and your mind is alive and you're trying to improve your poems technically, you will produce the work, and will never cease to produce it. In fact, I hope that with my last breath I shall make an addition to my technical equipment so that I will feel a little more satisfied to think of myself than I have been in the past. I think the older you get, provided you don't abuse your faculties, the better you're likely to be as an artist. (*GG*)

When you're through with sex, with ambition, what can an old man create? Art, of course, a piece of art that will go beyond him into the lives of young people, the people who haven't had time to create. The old man meets the young people and lives on. (*IW*, p. 22)

On Audience

Q. Do you think of yourself as writing for a definite audience?

A. No, I don't think of myself as writing for any definite audience. I write for a potential intelligence. I believe there's a bigger audience for what I write than ever gets to hear that I exist. In that I have lived a few years longer than formerly more people have come to read my stuff. . . . I believe also that there is a larger audience in general for unofficial writing than there was ten years ago. . . . This is, I believe, a slight edge of people in my own suburb for instance who are beginning vaguely to believe that a cubist, let us say, isn't for that a thief, a pervert and a dangerous communist. They even surreptitiously go to the public library and (when no one is looking) sneak my awful books out under their coats—and, I am told, snicker and chortle to themselves in their closets over what I have written saying, so I'm told, By God, that's true! (*Part R*, p. 42)

I've always wanted to fit poetry into the life around us because I love poetry. I'm not the type of poet who looks only at the rare thing. I want to use the words we speak and to describe the things we see, as far as it can be done. I abandoned the rare world of H.D. and Ezra Pound. Poetry should be brought into the world where we live and not be so recondite, so removed from the people. To bring poetry out of the clouds and down to earth I still believe possible. Using common words in a rare manner will advance the cause of the Poem infinitely. The world will be brought to share the wonders of the Poem. Poetry can be used to dignify life, which is so crass and vulgar. (*ND 17*, p. 253)

On T. S. Eliot

Interviewer: Do you still feel that the English influence on Eliot set us back twenty years?

Williams: Very definitely. He was a conformist. He wanted to go back to the iambic pentameter; and he did go back to it, very well; but he didn't acknowledge it. (*PR*, p. 15)

I paid attention very assiduously to what I was told. I often reacted violently, but I weighed what had been told me thoroughly. It was always my *own* mind I was making up. When I was halfway through the Prologue,[2] "Prufrock" appeared. I had a violent feeling that Eliot had betrayed what I believed in. He was looking backward; I was looking forward. He was a conformist, with wit, learning which I did not possess. He knew French, Latin, Arabic, God knows what. I was interested in that. But I felt he had rejected America and I refused to be rejected and so my reaction was violent. I realized the responsibility I must accept. I knew he would influence all subsequent American poets and take them out of my sphere. I had envisaged a new form of poetic composition, a form for the future. It was a shock to me that he was so tremendously successful; my contemporaries flocked to him—away from what I wanted. It forced me to be successful. (*IW*, p. 30)

It's all linked up in my mind with Eliot's walk-out on the liberal feelings of America, which I believe in. And in walking out he left modern poetry behind. The *Four Quartets* are very important to me. I look at them and at *The Waste Land* with great interest. *The Waste Land* was a bitter poem: he had not yet changed. . . . we were breaking the rules, whereas he was conforming to the excellencies of classroom English. He was writing poems as good as "The Ode to a Nightingale." They were effective, but we were writing poems from the dungheap—the Ashcan School. It is a fundamental difference in the structure of our thought, which was not Eliot's. He didn't want to get singed by getting too close to hell fire, with which we were playing. So he retreated from his position to save himself. (*T*)

On Image (and Imagism)

I was interested in the construction of an image before the image was popular in poetry. The poem "Metric Figure" is an example. I was influenced by my mother's still lifes. I was looking for a metric figure—a new measure. (*IW*, p. 21–22)

I utterly reject the metaphysical. "No ideas but in things." I reproved Marcia Nardi for using the term *God* without defining *God* in terms which can be understood by human beings. Look at the parables of Jesus—he didn't talk much of God, but he used simple examples—sheer poems! (*T*)

In telling the incidents that occurred to people, the story [3] of the lives of the people naturally unfolds. Without didactically telling what happened, you make things happen on the page, and from that you see what kind of people they were—what they suffered and what they aspired to. And that's what I hoped to do. I couldn't write—well, I really didn't want to write a didactic account of this that happened to that and that to another. I made the thing insofar as possible happen on the page. The imagistic method comes in there. You can't tell what a particular thing signified, but if you see the thing happening before you, you infer that that is the kind of thing that happens in the area. This is the imagistic method. (*ND 17*, p. 309)

On *In the American Grain*

By writing, writing, writing I did learn something. The approach to *In the American Grain* was my writing apprenticeship—my study period—studying grammar, syntax, spelling. The chapter that gave me the hardest job was the second voyage of Columbus—to tell the whole story and yet end at the end of the first voyage—that was a hard job. Waldo Frank called me up and said that technically, "The best thing you did was the construction of the first voyage." He was the only one to make a remark on the good construction of any of my pieces. (*T*)

On Intellect

The mind must be fed to keep it alert. . . . (*AS*, p. 455)

I believe the mind is the dominant force in the world today, the most valuable possession with which to face the world. . . . Without intelligence you can't judge any virtue in modern life. You have to make up your mind with your intelligence. When you speak of the intellect, that is something not quite acceptable to me. You can see the intelligence of a dog or the intellect of an Oppenheimer, but intelligence goes beyond technical ability. You have to judge intelligence by a man's total view of a situation, a political situation. Intelligence should be able to throw out the irrelevant parts of your life and to find what the particular parts of your life consist of. . . .

It is unintelligent to be taken in by blatant demagogy. You should be able to size up situations immediately to behave intelligently. (*T*)

On Measure

No action, no creative action is complete but a period from a greater action going in rhythmic course . . . . Imagination creates an image, point by point, piece by piece, segment by segment–into a whole, living. But each part as it plays into its neighbor, each segment into its neighbor segment and every part into every other, causing the whole–exists naturally in rhythm, and as there are waves there are tides and as there are ridges in the sand there are bars after bars . . . .

I do not believe in *vers libre*, this contradiction in terms.

Either the motion continues or it does not continue, either there is rhythm or no rhythm. *Vers libre* is prose. In the hands of Whitman it was a good tool, a kind of synthetic chisel—the best he had. In his bag of chunks even lie some of the pieces of rhythm life of which we must build. This is honor enough. *Vers libre* is finished—Whitman did all that was necessary with it. Verse has nothing to gain here and all to lose . . . .

Each piece of work, rhythmic in whole, is then in essence an assembly of tides, waves, ripples—in short, of greater and lesser rhythmic particles regularly repeated or destroyed. . . .

The rhythm unit is simply any repeated sequence of lengths and heights. Upon this ether the sounds are strung in their variety—slipping, clinging, overreaching, triumphing but always going forward even through moments of total disorder in the advance. Yet the rhythm persists, perfect . . . .

Here then, is the touchstone to it all: though the sounds of speech, i.e. words, letters, poetic lines, what not, convey the rhythm to a passion yet the rhythm itself is a thing apart and no sound. Upon this the wordy passions string sounds as they strain toward the perfect image. . . .

The one thing essential to rhythm is not sound but motion, of the two kinds: forward and up and down, rapidity of motion and quality of motion.

Thus the number of sounds in the rhythm unit do not because of their number give the unit any quality but only as they give motion in one of the two directions.

For this reason the poetic foot—dependent on the number of sounds composing it—cannot, except by chance, embody the rhythm unit. The motion might be given by either a greater or less number of sounds in the same unit.

By seeing the rhythm apart from the sounds clustering about it the old meter forms are enlarged into a unit more flexible and more accurate. And yet these meter forms, with their rigid stress and counted syllables, are a primitive perception of the true thing. But to count the syllables is but the bare makeshift for the appreciation of elapsing time. It is as stupid as to say that every musical measure in two-four time must contain only two notes.

Besides, how can syllables of no known length be taken three and three, five and five etc., and made into a unit of rhythm? I believe it impossible, no matter what the language, unless the rhythm is first put to music. . . .

In the new way:

The same rhythm, swift, may be of three syllables or if two are elided, of one: whereas, slow, it may consist of four or seven or any number that the sense agrees to. This is the flexibility that the modern requires . . . .

It presupposes a more finely attuned ear than has as yet been, a greater reserve, a quicker perception but in return it opens a way out of our word bound present. It opens a new field for the fine tools of accuracy now compelled to idleness and new places for masses that could not fit into the too rigid present forms. (*We*, pp. 82–83)

(Of "Asphodel"): My main aim is to break up the usual metrical pattern. In order to get away from the conventional thing, dividing it by breath, by inflection. I wanted to get away from everything that is English. (*T*)

It is the duty of the master to control his verse. Whitman made no attempt to control his verse, but he never knew what he was going to do. Not until the present day, when we considered relativity, were we able to control our verse, and all imitations of English verse are dead. The foot can no longer be considered fixed but relative. When we understand it we shall be able to control the line. (*T*)

The variable foot can be built along certain blocks of words. My method of work does not allow me to be didactic. I follow a certain loose pattern of verse, following three lines, allowing a certain relativistic foot. (*T*)

Yvor Winters was very partial to me, but he turned suddenly against me—much to my amazement. But I didn't care much if so much rigor mortis had set in. We were both interested in the American language, but I can't exactly put my finger on how close we were and how violently we separated. It had something to do with his feeling about free verse. He always said that one poem, "On the Road to the Contagious Hospital," he thought to be a perfect poem. He didn't retreat from that, but he didn't think I stuck enough to regularity, and after that he decided that I went off the trail. He wanted to go after the poem in a more formal way. But I couldn't see it. Twenty years ago I didn't know what I was doing. But it all hangs on the measure. I wanted to write in a colloquial way—not slang . . . I couldn't deform my lines to meet a formal pattern. It wasn't my conception of the thing at all. (*T*)

On Modern Poetry

The possibilities are infinite in our day. I don't believe about talk in the future. We are not men if we presume that the old boys were men and we're to go ahead and copy them. We then become mere replicas of the past and don't exist in our own right. It wouldn't be difficult for Braque to paint a Titian. But what would it be? Whereas, if Titian existed today he wouldn't be like Titian. He'd show us how to paint. Let's forget about the burden, the thought the poem might carry; and let's recognize the mechanism that can carry the sense, any sense. Think of Gertrude Stein: to use words as objects out of which you manufacture a little mechanism you call a poem which has to deliver the goods. That's what poetry must be.

I think we're succeeding to some extent in expressing what is in our own day. There is a much more intelligent interest in modern poetry now. It's been true for the last ten years. Probably it's the young instructors in the colleges. To say we're becoming crude is insane. Our poetry, our mechanisms, are much more delicate today. We're much more alert to life after a Freud and a Whitehead. (*B*)

I am a little concerned about the form. The art of the poem nowadays is something unstable, but at least the construction of the poem should make sense; you should know where you stand. Many questions haven't been answered as yet. Our poets may be wrong; but what can any of us do with his talent but try to develop his vision, so that through frequent failures we may learn better what we have missed in the past.

INTERVIEWER: What do you think you yourself have left of special value to the new poets?

WILLIAMS: The variable foot—the division of the line according to a new method that would be satisfactory to an American. It's all right if you are not intent on being national. But an American is forced to try to give the intonation. Either it *is* important or it is not important. It must have occurred to an American that the question of the line *was* important. The American idiom has much to offer us that the English language has never heard of. As for my own elliptic way of approach, it may be baffling, but it is not unfriendly, and not, I think, entirely empty. (*PR*, 29)

On Obscurity

Q. Why do we have to be so obscure?

A. Obscurity, once it is penetrated, is found to be a relatively simple matter. Obscurity is a very necessary impact to the listener and reader when anything really new is presented. The mind is conditioned to the past. Once a man has penetrated the obscure jungle he is likely to come out on the plateau where he has a much broader vision than he ever knew in the past.

When you think of Wagner (how he was damned!) and Ibsen, and, of course, many others! The term esoteric was first applied to Aristotle. (*B*, p. 101)

Q. Mr. Williams, the critics of poetry these days are other poets themselves. Isn't this because nobody but poets understand poetry any more?

A. I acknowledge that the difficulty of the poet's writing is a barrier to the public. Definitely. But I say he is forced to it in the modern world—to reflect the complexity of his thinking . . . . When I see a poet who's perfectly clear, I have to laugh.

Q. Why?

A. He isn't SAYING anything.

Q. You mean that you're only "saying" something when it's too obscure to be understood?

A. No. No. Not put that way. If a poem is read aloud, you may not understand completely what is being said, but you can have an emotional satisfaction which attracts you. (*MW*)

On Paterson

I always wanted to write a poem celebrating the local material . . . . I wanted to celebrate the material in a dignified way—not dignified, for heaven knows it was not dignified—but to use only the material that concerned the locale that I occupied, that I do occupy still, to have no connection with the European world, but to be purely American, to celebrate it as an American.

But it's hard to say how the idea was hatched. I had a concept that came to me: it was to speak as a person, as a certain person; and I thought to myself: "Well, if I am going to speak about a person it must be an actual person, but a really heroic figure as all epic poems are." But also a fanciful poem. It must be a fanciful poem, but dealing with particular events and a particular place. And I searched around for what would be the center of the thing. Because a city is a typical thing of the modern world, it's a place where men are most operative. You may think of individual men as being perhaps from a country district, but the concept of the city, as I conceived it, was man at his most accomplished. . . .

I wanted to get an image, an image which concerns all men, and yet a noble image. And the image of a city was necessary for me, the city of Paterson was most convenient. Because I knew most about the locale of that city, I chose it, deliberately chose it to write about. And as I came to look around, I found that it was very interesting in itself. It had a history, a colonial history, a very important one. . . . I wanted to write it in a way which would be characteristic not only of the place but of me. I started to make trips to the area. I walked around the streets; I went on Sundays in summer when the people were using the park, and I listened to their conversation as much as I could. I saw whatever they did, and made it part of the poem. (*ND 17*, 307–8)

INTERVIEWER: Did you ever think of using any other city as subject for a poem?

WILLIAMS: I didn't dare any mention of it in *Paterson*, but I thought strongly of Manhattan when I was looking about for a city to celebrate. I thought it was not particularized enough for me, not American in the sense I wanted. It was near enough, God knows, and I was familiar enough with it for all my purposes—but so was Leipzig, where I lived for a year when I was young, or Paris. Or even Vienna or even Frascati. But Manhattan escaped me.

INTERVIEWER: Someone remarks in one of these clippings that there is no reason the poem should ever end. Part Four completes the cycle, Five renews it. Then what?

WILLIAMS: [*laughing*] Go on repeating it. At the end—the last part, the dance—

INTERVIEWER: "We can know nothing but the dance . . ."

WILLIAMS: The dance.

To dance to a measure
contrapuntally,
Satyrically, the tragic foot.

That has to be interpreted; but how are you going to interpret it?

INTERVIEWER: I don't presume to interpret it; but perhaps the satyrs represent the element of freedom, of energy within the form.

WILLIAMS: Yes. The satyrs are understood as action, a dance. I always think of the Indians there. (*PR*, pp. 16–17)

On the Poem

We forget what a poem is: a poem is an organization of materials. As an automobile or kitchen stove is an organization of materials. You have to take words, as Gertrude Stein said we must, to make poems. Poems are mechanical objects made out of words to express a certain thing. (*GG*)

Q. Mr. Williams, can you tell me, simply, what poetry is?

A. Well . . . I would say that poetry is language charged with emotion. It's words, rhythmically organized . . . A poem is a complete little universe. It exists separately. Any poem that has worth expresses the whole life of the poet. It gives a view of what the poet is.

Q. All right, look at this part of a poem by E. E. Cummings, another great American poet:

(im) c-a-t (mo)
b, i; l: e
FalleA
ps! fl
Oattumbll
sh? dr
lftwhirlF
  (Ul) (lY)
&&&

Is *this* poetry?

A. I would reject it as a poem. It may be, to him, a poem. But I would reject it. I can't understand it. He's a serious man, so I struggle very hard with it—and I get no meaning at all.

Q. You get no meaning? But here's a part of a poem you yourself have written: . . . "2 partridges / 2 mallard ducks / a Dungeness crab / 24 hours out / of the Pacific / and 2 live-frozen / trout / from Denmark . . ."[4] Now, that sounds just like a fashionable grocery list!

A. It is a fashionable grocery list.

Q. Well—is it poetry?

A. We poets have to talk in a language which is not English. It is the American idiom. Rhythmically, it's organized as a sample of the American idiom. It has as much originality as jazz. If you say, "2 partridges, 2 mallard ducks, a Dungeness crab"—if you treat that rhythmically, ignoring the practical sense, it forms a jagged pattern. It is, to my mind, poetry.

Q. But if you don't "ignore the practical sense" . . . you agree that it's a fashionable grocery list?

A. Yes. Anything is good material for poetry. Anything. I've said it time and time again.

Q. Aren't we supposed to understand it?

A. There is a difference between the essence of poetry and the sense. Sometimes modern poets ignore the sense completely. That's what makes some of the difficulty . . . The audience is confused by the shape of the words.

Q. But shouldn't a word mean something, when you see it?

A. In prose, an English word means what it says. In poetry, you're listening to two things . . . you're listening to the sense, the common sense of what it says. But it says more. That is the difficulty. (*MW*)

On His Own Poems, 1956 to 1961 (T)

On "The Avenue of Poplars": I was writing in my own language, and whatever the language suggested I wrote. I was following the beat in my own mind, the beat of the American idiom.

On "To a Solitary Disciple": I was sure there'd be one . . . .

On "Sunday": As Ezra says: "The poet must always be writing, even when he has nothing to write about—just for discipline." Much as Richard Strauss wrote his "Domestic Symphony," which I heard in Germany in 1910. Why not write a symphony using the noises in a house? And I put this feeling into this poem—just finger exercises.

On "The Trees": I was trying to get speed in verse—not time enough in the modern world to be prolix. I was feeling for an impetuous rhythm, a Declaration of Independence from every restraint.

On "View of a Lake": I was inclined to trust the sequence of rhythm without punctuation. It was the Image, the significant Image, that made the poem. To put down something as a composition—not a story, not in the stanzaic form. To be something of what I saw—the three little bitches gaping at the stalled traffic. I felt more kinship with them than with the stalled traffic. I was as much with the kids as with another animal. I never thought it was a very good poem but I liked it.

On "The Wanderer": This was the genesis of *Paterson* and started as the idealization of my grandmother, Mrs. Wellcome. . . . The figure of my grandmother in "The Wanderer" was semimythical. You must remember that I had been reading Keats's *Hyperion* and *Aucassin & Nicolette*. It must have started with the long poem, a romance, during medical school. Bocklin's *Insel des Todes* started that when I was in Germany. A fantastic story of a prince who at a wedding feast had been drugged so that he was dragged out by his nurse. He was to have been married to a beautiful girl. Half unconscious he had been transported to a foreign country. His whole desire was to get home. That is the poem I took to Arlo Bates, whose comments sent me home to destroy the poem.

In "The Wanderer" I identified my grandmother with my poetic unconscious. She was the personification of poetry. I wanted to identify myself with something good and philosophical—with a perfect knowledge of the world. I thought of myself as all-good and all-wise. So the grandmother, who was the spirit of the river, led to the Passaic. The Wanderer was a disappointed, a defeated person—myself. Then came *Paterson*, a greater realization of immediate surroundings. I rejected "The Wanderer" because it was too stilted, too romantic. I read Byron's *Don Juan* with the cleverness of which I was fascinated. I was also full of Pound and his classical attempts. But he identified with Provence and the old world, whereas I wanted to do my own country. Keats I found beautiful, but he was not for me. I wanted to do it my way and be beautiful at the same time.

On "Winter Sunset": The hopeless feeling that comes over me on a winter day. That is why I'm a poet setting poetry against a hopeless nature. I'm a pessimist and I must lift myself up by my bootstraps. My mother was a moody person, and her moods affected me.

On "The Young Housewife": Whenever a man sees a beautiful woman it's an occasion for poetry—compensating beauty with beauty.

On the Poet

Actually the poet is the happiest of men. He may be stimulated to an extent by unhappiness, though also by happiness. I think that basic faith in the world, and actual love for the world, that is, to sum up: happiness—is the basic ground of a poet's makeup. I don't think unhappiness makes you sing at all, or makes you want to construct something. . . . The man must have an interest, he must have a desire, he must have a passion to make something better in the world than what he sees about him. He is a poet, therefore he is a word-user. He makes something out of his poems. That comes from a desire to build something useful—an affection for his fellow men, his kind. I think that is where the modern poet, in the best sense, differs from his romantic, despairing confreres of the past. We know that we have a big job to do. Our political and philosophical organization is sometimes anything but what we desire. Therefore, let the hopeful artist manufacture of the materials of his art something—although it may not be recognized by the ordinary person—which will be an organization of materials on a better basis than it had been before. It is the job of the workman-artist to manufacture a better world than he sees—and he only does that if he feels that it's worth doing, and therefore he's an optimist. He believes in his world, he believes in his people, and that's the reason he's a poet. (*GG*)

Who are the best poets of our day? I am not going to attempt to name them. In my opinion there are not many. . . . Their work has been long in ripening. Vergil's [*sic*] pear tree had something of that same fruit. My will to go on with my life is enmeshed in the determination to contribute all I am worth for this. When I am convinced that I have contributed something to the art of the poem, the total poem, the poem as it did not exist before I was born, I am happy in my innermost heart and continue happy for days or months at a time, or as long as I can continue in this belief.

This stimulates me, drives me with inexorable fire to go on. Without this feeling of happiness, or the possibility of it, I would not write another word. But granted this drive constantly uppermost in my mind, I cannot quit.

This is a drive which I cannot but salute. It seems eminently selfish. It is not. For among the men and women whom I salute are certain individuals who are worth more than anything I myself can attain, no matter how I may try. (*AS*, pp. 453–54)

On Politics in Relation to Poetry

I lost faith in what can happen in the world—no specific betrayal. It was pretty obvious that the world wasn't going to right itself after World War I. We kept hoping that something would happen. It is the idealist who is finally thrown for a loss. I was thoroughly disillusioned. I was full of ideals, whatever they are. If you talk of forms of government, they are all opportunistic. I wasn't a communist, for I knew nothing about it, but I was anticapitalistic.

Government was made up of weak men. I don't think any government is worth much. Nothing doing for a Plato's government by intelligence—it won't work. There's nothing to do but put yourself aside and live your life. Intelligence always has to give way to the masses. Self-effacement, which is a despairing way, is the only way. Get on with your fellowmen as best you can. . . . I believe the characteristics of the age help your writing when you go along with them. I may be pig-headed about that, but I believe that the age should govern what you write. You should be alert to the age. (*T*)

Q. How would you describe the political tendency of American writing as a whole since 1930?

A. The political tendency of American writing as a whole since 1930 and thirty years before has been toward a discovery of the terms of a discussion and declaration in the only world it can know, that under its nose. When it has succeeded in knowing what it is talking about in those terms it may possibly begin to interest the man of alert senses (Henry Adams) who already knows the world but would be glad to see it correlated by the artist (the writer) in some new sort of creative composition. "Literary nationalism" [5] is a confusion in terms due to bandy-legged and cross-eyed witnesses to what is before them. It hides under its blatancies the very much neglected fact that when a man sees and apprehends with his mind what is before him in America that which he sees there must perforce be American. Give stupidity any name you please, call it American, British, or even German, it's still stupidity. We're not talking about that. A renewed interest in specifically "American" elements in our culture (provided they are related in the mind to general culture) would be the beginning of any basic understanding of literature among us.

Q. Have you considered the question of your attitude toward the possible entry of the United States into the next world war? What do you think the responsibilities of writers in general are when and if war comes?

A. If war comes we've got to fight. Writing would be secondary. The one thing to guard against would be the tendency to become a liar for propaganda's sake. That difficulty always faces a man. If I had to be shot, I'd hope fervently that the guys at the other end would make an artistic job of it by shooting straight. The value always comes out, in one form or another, if we stick to our guns. Meanwhile, long live in America the memory of Eugene Debs! (*Part R*, pp. 43–44)

INTERVIEWER: Not to mention political matters. Edgar [6] says that in the political club which your father started, you were always the liberal. . . .

MRS. WILLIAMS: I think Bill has always been willing to be reckless. There was the social credit business for instance, that Bill got involved in in the thirties. They wanted to give a kind of dividend to the people to increase purchasing power. There were large meetings in New York and down at the University of Virginia. But that was about the end of it. In fact many of those involved withdrew from it when they saw how things were going, with the war coming on and all. Some of them were so nervous about that whole episode they wouldn't even speak to Bill. That's the difference. I don't say Bill was naïve; perhaps it was honesty. Bill isn't a radical or a communist or anything else. He's an honest man. And if he gets into it with both feet, it's just too bad. That's the way it's been.[7] (*PR*, p. 24)

On Ezra Pound

I've always loved that guy. He was and is one of the most sympathetic human beings. I've just written him that he was one of the first to write in the American idiom. He couldn't get away from it. (*T*)

Pound gave me the original lesson: Never use two words where one will do. (*T*)

When I was at the University of Pennsylvania, around 1905, I used to argue with Pound. I'd say "bread" and he'd say "caviar." It was a sort of simplification of our positions. Once, in 1912 I think it was, in a letter (we were still carrying on our argument) he wrote, "all right, bread." But I guess he went back to caviar. (*B*)

On Rhyme

Very early I began to question whether to rhyme and decided: No. I . . . found I couldn't say what I had to say in rhyme. It got in my way . . . . You can see the exact spot in the early poems where I quit rhyme. I began to begin lines with lower-case letters. I thought it pretentious to begin every line with a capital letter. These two decisions, not to rhyme and to begin lines with lower-case letters, were made very early. The decisions lasted all the rest of my life. (*IW*, pp. 14–15)

On Short Stories

INTERVIEWER: Did you write the short stories on a different "level" than the poems—as a kind of interlude to them?

WILLIAMS: No, as an alternative. They were written in the form of a conversation which I was partaking in. We were in it together.

INTERVIEWER: Then the composition of them was just as casual and spontaneous as you have suggested. You would come home in the evening and write twelve pages or so without revising?

WILLIAMS: I think so. I was coming *home*. I was placing myself in continuation of a common conversation . . . . Reality. Reality. My vocabulary was chosen out of the intensity of my concern. When I was talking in front of a group, I wasn't interested in impressing them with my power of speech, but only with the seriousness of my intentions toward them. I had to make them come alive. (*PR*, pp. 8–9)

On Tradition

Q. Are you conscious, in your own writing, of the existence of a "usable past"? Is this mostly American? What figures would you designate as elements in it?

A. Yes, most assuredly, I am conscious in everything I write of a usable past, a past as alive in its day as every moment is today alive in me: Work therefore as different from mine as one period can be different from another, but in spite of that preserving between the two an identity upon which I feed. In all work in any period there is a part that is the life of it which relates to whatever else is alive, yesterday, today, and forever. To discover that in past work makes that work important to me. How can we say that the work of Henry James is more relevant to the present and future of American writing than the writing of Walt Whitman, or vice versa? The only question of any relevance in either case is, Was that work alive to its own day? If so then it is alive every day. If it was a palpable denial of its own day then—if I can discover it as such—out with it. I want to look in a work and see in it a day like my own, of altered shapes, colors, but otherwise the same. *That* I can use to reinforce my senses and my intelligence to go on discovering in my own day such things as those old boys had the courage and intelligence to discover in theirs. Let's omit the matter of art, the art, that is, to set down what they saw and experienced and DIDN'T lie about—for any reason. (*Part R*, 41–42)

Q. Do you find, in retrospect, that your writing reveals any allegiance to any group, class, organization, region, . . . or do you conceive of it as mainly the expression of yourself as an individual?

A. In retrospect my writing reveals plenty of allegiances—to the grammar-school ideals of my public-school bringing up. You know, no sooner a child is born than he begins to learn. I was early indoctrinated into the gang spirit of my eight- and ten-year-old pals. I have never forgotten that thrilling world with all its magnificent hopes and determinations. Me and Dante loved at the age of—well, anyway she was about nine at the time. . . . There were things I learned in my father's own Unitarian Sunday School to which I owe the staunchest allegiance today. Then I have been tremendously impressed with the past of the United States. That's deep in my blood. Nothing has displaced one bit of my emotion—the regular Fourth of July stuff! that I once felt so strongly. In my world there are no classes but the good guys and the bastards. No, I don't think of my writing as the expression merely of an individual, never. Who the hell am I? But I am passionately one, not of a writers' group, but with a potential right-feeling and thinking man of the world, the kernel of all groups, the best one in all times and places, whom I conceive of as having patience, tolerance, no prejudices whatever but a keen sense for values. I still believe that such men can get along together in peace and work out a livable world. If not, there's little meaning to the whole business. (*Part R*, p. 43)

I came to look at poetry from a local viewpoint; I had to find out for myself; I'd had no instruction beyond high-school literature. When I was inclined to write poems, I was very definitely an American kid, confident of himself and also independent. From the beginning I felt I was *not* English. (*IW*, p. 14)

On Writing

Q. What would you say about the mental and physical condition of the poet? What is his condition when he writes his best work?

A. It doesn't make any difference where he is—whether he's alone, as some might like to be, or whether he's in the next room, as Mozart liked to be with a dance going on, writing independently, and feeling alone. Certainly when he writes, he is feeling intensely himself, in whatever place he happens to be. And, I'm sufficient of a doctor to know that no one can do any good work unless the supply of oxygen to his brain is so intense that he can do his best work. In my case it's not in a dreamy, relaxed state whatever, but in a tense state, that the best work occurs. It might be when you're fatigued. Perhaps fatigue is an anesthetic, lets the body go to some unimportant place, lets the faculties come out sharply and dominate the whole psychosomatic picture. I think the psychic element must dominate, and your body be secondary, but tense.

Q. Usually the best work has already been done, when the poet was younger. From your own experience, what would you say about the age most conducive to the writing of poetry?

A. Naturally, the type of poetry that is written by a man —or the type of *poem* (I dislike the term *poetry*—I speak of poems only)—the type of poems naturally will vary according to the man's age. It depends entirely on what your interest in the poem is. If you're trying to construct a work that will be comparable in interest to the major scientific and philosophic interests of your day, you will be more likely to do satisfactory work as you grow older. If you're writing a love lyric, it's possible that the intensity of a love passion might inspire a certain rhythmic construction which could be called a poem. But *why* is it a poem? . . . .

Q. With your own work, is the first draft of a poem final, as it appears in print, or are there subsequent stages of revision and repairing?

A. Everything happens. Some poems are written down and never changed. I've written eight or ten poems—let's agree that they're poems—written them down without touching a word; I do it every once in a while. For example such a poem as "The Yachts" was written right off without changing a word; some other poems I have jotted down, rejected them and returned to them as late as a year or two afterward and completed them. Sometimes I became completely stuck and not able to go ahead with them at all, and had to reject them, that's true. So: everything happens. In general, the most spontaneous bits of poems are written right off, quickly, from a subconscious or unconscious self and it just does actually pour out without the knowledge of the man who writes it. But, the better artist he is, the better he's able to recognize what is good and *why* it's good—and how to organize it into a satisfactory poem. He must have his theories, as Pasteur said, he must work to them, and so he becomes what has been termed in the past a master—a man who knows what everything means, knows why he put it down, can take it apart and put it together again and still have it as spontaneous as ever. In fact, Yeats said you must labor to be beautiful. (*GG*)

I don't need to imitate. I have to make my own way. But I can't be pushed aside. The old beginners had to make their own way. They didn't need to copy any master, and we don't need to copy a master. When the urge to speak comes on a person he does not think of a master.

Shyness is the very thing that makes you speak. You can't speak with your own voice in a dramatic situation, so you write it. (*T*)

When I start writing, I put on the heat . . . . May do it late at night or early in the morning. (*PMC*)

Q. Do you place much value on the criticism your work has received?

A. I place no value at all on the criticism my work has received if the puerilities of public statement . . . are in question. But I have received extremely valuable criticisms by word of mouth from the same gentlemen who write often so stalely of me in the papers. Most criticism is first poised to praise or to injure before the man thinks. We are all guilty. Few know what writing is about. Those that do, find little or no audience for what they have to say. (*Part R*, p. 42)

On Women

The thing that keeps me interested in life after having driven through to whatever success I have been able to attain among my fellow men is, obviously enough, the women. Women still have something to sell me. Take a young woman I saw only yesterday at a reading. What eyes! Not that they were so beautiful in a magazine-cover sense—there was something else, something any man would be proud to have evoked in a woman's eyes were he on the brink of the grave. You can't buy that.

Women are more sensitive to what Ezra Pound once called "the purring of the invisible antennae." There are, of course, whores—poor girls, if they don't want to rob you or stick you with a knife. But these are not the creatures

I'm talking about. Even when women are old, and sometimes very old, they still retain, if they are aware, something I still find worth my while digging for. When I am asked why I find life worth living, it is the look in the woman's eyes that I saw yesterday which rescues me with an answer.

I'm not vain—it's long past the time for that. Maybe it's a memory, but I don't think so. Love was never as sweet as that. I'm not sorry for myself, for I think I can lie down in my bed and die as uncomplaining as any man, as my father did under similar circumstances. . . . life still interests me, and not because of any masculine competition. Let my sex take care of themselves. But the gentleness and tenderness and insight and loyalty of women and what they see, I am sure, in most masculine looks which should disgust them, keep me plugging. (*AS*, 456–57)

III
Memoir and Miscellany

Gael Turnbull's reminiscence of a 1958 visit with the Williamses originally appeared in *Mica 3* (June 1961). It catches perfectly the deep charity and enthusiasm with which visitors—particularly young or aspiring writers—were welcomed. As such people as Robert Bly, Denise Levertov, Robert Lowell, Allen Ginsberg, James Wright, Richard Emerson, Robert Wallace, David Ignatow, Galway Kinnell, Robert Creeley, and countless other writers would agree, Williams's "speaking straight ahead" remains a most touching and cherished memory. Williams's own "How to Write" and "The American Idiom" are concise statements of his views on language, education, and modern poetry. The former was published in the very first issue of *New Directions in Prose and Poetry* (1936), the latter in the seventeenth number of the same anthology series (1961).

A Visit to WCW: September, 1958

From the Diary of Gael Turnbull

SUNDAY I phoned Rutherford. The silliness of it, to make sure that I had him and not his son. Then my name. Instantly he knew it. A childish excitement. "Well, now . . . well, now . . . if that doesn't . . . so where are . . . My, my!" And so, settled that we were to go the next afternoon.

The chaos of cars, noises, down the canyons between the skyscrapers, to roar through the Lincoln Tunnel under the river (like a packet in a vacuum tube). Out on a maze of overpasses and expressways, dodging the big cars. Out, out, in a landscape of factories and desolate wastes, where a man seemed an impertinence.

Then a sign: Rutherford, and abruptly we were in a "small town," trees, grassy lawns, white frame houses, quiet main street, parking meters, tucked away, gentle. (And yet, only a few moments ago, looking back in the rear mirror I had seen the whole skyline of New York, terrible in the sun, military, metallic, Cyclopean.)

To find Ridge Road. And number nine, it is almost on the main street, practically at the town center. Workmen hammering, boards lying about. A woman coming out (patient? or son's wife?) to direct us in over the sawdust. Bill (the son) having an afternoon surgery, camped out in the dining room because of the construction. A few women with children. Paintings on the wall, Ben Shahn one.

Then WCW down the stairs. Shorter than I'd thought, and more stocky. Thinning white hair and prominent nose. Fussy and happy. Reached out with both hands to take Jonnie's and mine at once. "So you are here . . . I can't believe . . . This is wonderful . . ."

Then into the drawing room, I talking a bit nervously. To sit . . . "Just sit for a minute and *look* at each other." And so we looked, all of us grinning, and his eyes twinkling. Moving a little restlessly, but no sign of any paralysis. Kind face, an old man, showing a certain sinking of the flesh, a sort of withdrawal.

And then after he had surveyed us to his satisfaction, we went around the room looking at the paintings. By his brother Ed . . . and his own mother . . . .

Then Floss came, thinner than WCW, and somehow looking physically stronger. She gives a sense that he, and poetry, and the whole world, are a queer sort of show that she never really had anticipated; but once it had all happened, she'd go along with it and take part and enjoy it, and observe with a certain wry humor, a kind of reserve, but not aloof really.

So we went upstairs to his study, and we talked the usual things, about our trip over, and being in New York, etc. etc. Sometimes he'd say things that it was hard to quite catch, half-finished phrases, and a nervous speed of voice. It was as if he had opened his mind to you completely, every disconnected fragment that came into his mind.

Then he brings a copy of *Paterson Five*, all ready and inscribed for me, and he says he hopes I'll find something interesting in it (and the humility, that he really isn't very confident, and to think that I would like something in it would be a great pleasure to him). Then I feel desperate, that he should do so, and give him a drawing of mine, the one of the heraldic beast, the Lion of St. Mark (and this because it is my *own* favorite, and so, in giving it, I feel the greatest loss myself, and hence the greatest satisfaction in the act). And he is duly impressed by its ferocity.

He has just written a poem (*The Nation* asked for one) so he shows it to me, "Now, what do you think of it? I don't know."

The poem is called "Advice to Mr. Eliot" and it is just that. He urges me, truly concerned, "Now, what *do* you think of it?" Nervously, wanting my approval (yes, I wasn't indulging my fancy, I know that, he wanted my opinion and my approval, or anyone's). And under his eyes, the sudden desperate intent, I can do nothing but say what is in my mind, I can't escape the commitment, "I don't like the last two lines. I'd like it better if you stopped here." Pointing at the sheet. And he looks too, and nods, and nods again, "Yes, yes, so you do think so? Well, maybe you're right. Maybe. I don't know. I'll have to see about it. I wonder. You are probably right. But I don't know." And he looks a little crestfallen, but only the slightest bit, while I squirm inwardly, trapped by his sincerity.

Then I mention having heard of the "work room" he used to have and he takes me up to the attic, a bit awkward on the stairs, a typical old attic, but large. "We used to have parties here. Oh, those were wild days! In the twenties and thirties. People would come out here. Drink and girls. We'd goose them from behind as we came up the stairs." And he'd grin, like an impudent urchin . . .

And all the old magazines and books, and bits of unfinished manuscripts, and all that is left of his writing boards are two or three rickety bits. "I used to have a stove up here, and a telephone, so I could come up and stay here as long as I wanted. I had to get away."

"But it's all gone now. Let's go back to the study. They can get rid of all this junk once I'm dead." Then he talks of Rutherford . . . No bars. And medicine. "I never had any contact with anyone here. I couldn't live their life. I used to hate it. A poet shouldn't have to live!"—savagely without more explanation and as if it were perfectly obvious. . . .

And then later, "I don't know what it is. It was as if there was a devil in me. I think I believe in the devil. Something in me, that kept at me, wouldn't let me alone, wouldn't let me rest." And then, again, about women, "Oh, Floss, what she's put up with. I don't know how. I was pretty raw in those days. Some of the women, too. It was all wrong. But there it is. I wonder what she thinks of me."

And then, "But we're old now. We're just in the way.

The sooner we're gone, the better. We should let Bill take over the house." And then, "I've always felt so lost here, this town, I wanted to get out, I couldn't stick it, so I had to write, you see, there wasn't anything else I suppose. And now my life is gone."

Then, suddenly, we are talking so intimately that I am frightened, and want to escape, he saying, "I wonder what good it's been . . ." and I say, "You've given part of your life to me. Maybe that's all we can ever do with our lives, give some to someone else." And he nods, "Yes, yes, that's it." And I can feel his death which is the last little bit of all the actions we call living, an old man and a young man; and it is intolerable.

So that abruptly he says, "But let's not talk like this. Let's go down in the garden." And he smiles again, and moves off restlessly, and I'm glad to go.

He has trouble to read, and can only do it with labor, and even a book on his desk will be hard to find again once put down. And he asks about England, and about Tomlinson, and tells of how he was put through some tests at Berkeley by some psychologists who were investigating the "creative genius," and grins happily, childishly, "Oh, I gave them their money's worth. Oh, I really put it on. Some of the things I said! Well, they asked for it, so they could have it. I don't care, not any more."

We spoke of Allen Ginsberg and of Cid Corman; and he spoke out of deep feeling and warmth, and pity too, for their struggles. And Floss told of old parties, of Max Bodenheim who came to scrounge off them, and who announced the first evening that he couldn't eat carrots under any circumstances. And she said, "So I made damn sure I served him carrots the very next meal, and he ate them too!" She didn't have much opinion of him, anyway. I could sense that some of WCW's friends, of this kind, had been more than a slight barb between them.

So we talked on, about nothing much, gossip mostly, as if we had been old neighbors . . . And then we thought of my car, and the parking meter ". . . I've got a nickel here for the meter. Go on. Go on. They'll catch you if they can."

I remark on a huge boulder, about half my height, standing in the bushes. "Oh, that was dug up when they were putting in the foundations for the place across the street. I asked if I could have it. I don't know why I wanted it. But I got it. They thought I was crazy."

And he looked around at the street, the American small-town street, spacious, with trees and lawns; and in the autumn now, thick with scattered leaves. "It's not my life, but I couldn't get out. I don't know how it could be otherwise. It must be different in England." And I can sense it, and am appalled, that *he* should feel isolated and cut off, he of all people, and I say, "Then indeed, if *you* feel that, if you do, then there is hope for all and any of us." Then he shakes his head, and moves restlessly back to the house, as if to show that he didn't mean me to take him seriously.

We go through where they are rebuilding the new surgery and waiting room for his son. He is at times critical of it, and then unsure. "D'you think the steps are too big? I mean, for mothers with children?"

I can see that he is tired, the strain of a visitor makes him nervous, and we gather ourselves to go. We squeeze their hands, and they hold the children for a moment, and we say all the usual things that one does say, and mean all of them.

He says, "I don't suppose we'll ever see you again. It's always like that. All our friends." And I want to deny it, I want to say, "But of course we'll see you again," and I want to say that we'll be back soon. But I know that what he says is true, that we may quite probably not see each other again, and I drive away very quickly down the main street, seeing the sign "Rutherford" by a bank, to get away, because it's all that I can do not to cry, and that's very stupid somehow.

But, equally, proud that I want to cry. For if there be

nothing in life worth such tears, just to say good-by, then indeed we have nothing.

So back into New York, back into the traffic, and the tall buildings, in the early evening, still light, still hearing their voices in our ears, while the taxis crash past on every side and I wonder if I'll ever be able to find a place to park.

How to Write

William Carlos Williams

ONE TAKES a piece of paper, anything, the flat of a shingle, slate, cardboard and with anything handy to the purpose begins to put down the words after the desired expression in mind. This is the anarchical phase of writing. The blankness of the writing surface may cause the mind to shy, it may be impossible to release the faculties. Write, write anything: it is all in all probability worthless anyhow, it is never hard to destroy written characters. But it is absolutely essential to the writing of anything worth while that the mind be fluid and release itself to the task.

Forget all rules, forget all restrictions, as to taste, as to what ought to be said, write for the pleasure of it—whether slowly or fast—every form of resistance to a complete release should be abandoned.

For today we know the meaning of depth, it is a primitive profundity of the personality that must be touched if what we do is to have it. The faculties, untied, proceed backward through the night of our unconscious past. It goes down to the ritualistic, amoral past of the race, to fetish, to dream to wherever the "genius" of the particular writer finds itself able to go.

At such a time the artist (the writer) may well be thought of as a dangerous person. Anything may turn up. He has no connection with ordered society. He may perform an imbecility or he may by a freak of mind penetrate with tremendous value to society into some avenue long closed or never yet opened. But he is disconnected with any orderly advance or purpose.

It is now that artists stoutly defend themselves against any usefulness in their art. And it makes no difference whether it is a treatise on mathematics or a poem that is being written. *While* it is being written, as far as possible, the writer be he mathematician or poet, must with a stored mind no doubt, must nevertheless thoroughly abandon himself to the writing in greater or less degree if he wishes to clinch his expression with any depth of significance.

The demonic power of the mind is its racial and individual past, it is the rhythmic ebb and flow of the mysterious life process and unless this is tapped by the writer nothing of moment can result. It is the reason for the value of poetry whose unacknowledged rhythmic symbolism is its greatest strength and which makes all prose in comparison with it little more than the patter of the intelligence.

So poets have been considered unbalanced creatures (as they often are), madmen very often. But the intrinsic reason for this is seldom understood. They are in touch with "voices," but this is the very essence of their power, the voices are the past, the depths of our very beings. It is the deeper, not "lower" (in the usually silly sense) portions of the personality speaking, the middle brain, the nerves, the glands, the very muscles and bones of the body itself speaking.

But once the writing is on the paper it becomes an object. It is no longer a fluid speaking through a symbolism of ritualistic forms but definite words on a piece of paper. It has now left the region of the formative past and come up to the present. It has entered now a new field, that of intelligence. I do not say that the two fields do not somewhat overlap at times but the chief characteristic of the writing now is that it is an object for the liveliest attention that the full mind can give it and that there has been a change in the whole situation.

It is this part of writing that is dealt with in the colleges and in all forms of teaching but nowhere does it seem to be realized that without its spring from the deeper strata of the personality all the teaching and learning in the world can make nothing of the result. Not to have realized this is the greatest fault of those who think they know something of the art.

All that the first phase of writing has accomplished is to place its record on the paper. Is this valuable, is it worthless? These questions it cannot answer and it is of no use for the poet to say: This is what *I* have done, therefore it is excellent. He may say that and what he has done may be excellent but the reasons should be made clear and they involve the conscious intelligence.

The written object comes under the laws of all created things involving a choice and once the choice has been made there must be an exercise of the will to back it. One goes forward carefully. But the first step must not be to make what has been written under a quasi-hallucinatory state conform to rules. What rules? Rather the writing should be carefully examined for the new and the extraordinary and nothing rejected without clear reason. For in this way the intelligence itself is corrected.

Thus, we know that in language is anchored most or all of the wisdom and follies of our lives. Besides which language may grow stale, meanings may and will be lost, phrases may block our arrival at conclusion. And in the writings of genius, in the poems (if any) the released personality of the artist the very break with stupidity which we are seeking may have occurred. And this will always be in the *form* which that first writing has taken.

But lest a mistake occur I am not speaking of two persons, a poet and a critic, I am speaking of the same person, the writer. He has written with his deepest mind, now the object is there and he is attacking it with his most recent mind, the forebrain, the seat of memory and ratiocination, the so-called intelligence.

This cannot do more in reviewing that which is before it than reject that which has been said better elsewhere. Whereas in the first phase a man need not seriously have written at all, now it is necessary that he know the work of other men, in other times, as much as possible and from every available angle. This is the student's moment.

And for an American there is one great decision to be made. What language is being written?

A few years ago some American in England wrote an attack upon American writers living in America saying in effect; How can they write English not hearing it spoken every day?—His comment was meant to be ironical but it turned out to be naïve. The answer to his question is, naturally: Why bother with English when we have a language of our own?

It is the intelligence which gives us the history of writing and its point of arrival today, the place of Poe, the value of Whitman, the purpose of free verse, why it occurred at just that time, the significance of Gertrude Stein's work, that of the writings of James Joyce and the rationale of modern verse structure.

Briefly all this is the birth of a new language. It is a new allotment of significance. It is the cracking up of phrases which have stopped the mind.

All these things could be gone into in detail, a book could be written and must be written of them, but that is not my purpose here. What I have undertaken is to show the two great phases of writing without either of which the work accomplished can hardly be called mastery. And that, in the phrase of James Joyce, is the he and the she of it.

The American Idiom

William Carlos Williams

THE AMERICAN IDIOM is the language we speak in the United States. It is characterized by certain differences from the language used among cultured Englishmen, being completely free from all influences which can be summed up as having to do with "the Establishment." This, pared to essentials, is the language which governed Walt Whitman in his choice of words. It constituted a revolution in the language. (In France, only Paul Fort recognized what had happened about him to negate the *Académie*.)

The language had been deracinated in this country, but the English tongue was a tough customer with roots bedded in a tradition of far-reaching cultural power. Every nursery rhyme gave it a firmer grip on the tradition and there were always those interested in keeping their firm hold upon it.

Every high school in America is duty bound to preserve the English language as a point of honor, a requirement of its curriculum. To fail in *English* is unthinkable!

Ignoring the supreme masters of English composition and thinking to go beyond them along the same paths impugns a man's loyalty if not his good sense. In fact, it has been baldly stated in the highest circles and believed that there is no American language at all—so low have we fallen in defense of our speech.

The result is a new and unheralded language which has grown stronger by osmosis, we are asked to believe, but actually by the power of those Whitmans among us who were driven to take a chance by their fellows and the pride of an emerging race, its own. The American idiom had been driven into a secondary place by our scholars, those rats that had abandoned it to seek salvage elsewhere in safer places. No one can blame them, no one can say that we shall survive to plant our genes in another world.

We must go forward—uncertainly it may be, but courageously as we may. Be assured that measure in mathematics as in verse is inescapable; so in reply to the fixed foot of the ancient line, including the Elizabethans, we must have a reply: it is the variable foot which we are beginning to discover after Whitman's advent.

"The Establishment," fixed in its commitments, has arrived at its last stand: the iambic pentameter, blank verse, the verse of Shakespeare and Marlowe which give it its prestige. A full stop. Until we can go beyond that, "the Establishment" has an edge on us.

Whitman lived in the nineteenth century but he, it must be acknowledged, proceeded instinctively by rule of thumb and a tough head, correctly, in the construction of his verses. He knew nothing of the importance of what he had stumbled on, unconscious of the concept of the variable foot. This new notion of time which we were approaching, leading to the work of Curie and the atom bomb, and other *new* concepts have been pregnant with far-reaching consequences.

We were asleep to the tremendous responsibilities—as poets and as writers generally—that were opening up to us. Our poets especially are asleep from the neck down—only the Russians with their state control of letters are stupider than we. And still we follow the English and teach it to our unsuspecting children.

Notes

I—Interviews

Notes by Emily Wallace

1 William George Williams, 1851–1918.

2 Raquel Hélène Rose Hoheb Williams, 1847–1949.

3 Edgar Irving Williams, 1884–1974, was a distinguished architect.

4 Williams's *Selected Essays* is dedicated: "To the memory of 'Uncle' Billy Abbott / the first English teacher / who ever gave me an / A."

5 Morrison Robb Van Cleve and Ezra Pound were in the chorus of captive Greek maidens in *Iphigenia among the Taurians,* presented in April of 1903 under the direction of the Department of Greek, with music composed by Professor Hugh Archibald Clarke. Williams and Hilda Doolittle were in the audience.

6 The first meeting occurred in the fall of 1902. Although Pound transferred to Hamilton College the following year, he visited his friend during vacations, and he returned to the University in 1905 as a graduate student in Romanics and received an M.A. in 1906 at the same commencement that Williams was awarded his M.D. degree.

7 William Eric Williams was born January 7, 1914, and Paul Herman Williams, September 13, 1916. Quite probably Williams is laughing to himself about another "baby," Florence Herman Williams; if "today" is June 18, it is the "monthiversary" (a word he coined) of his wife's birthday, April 18.

8 Although *The Tempers* was published in 1917 during World War I, Williams here must mean *The Wedge,* published in 1944, which has an introductory essay beginning: "The war is the first and only thing in the world today. The arts generally are not, nor is this writing a diversion from that for relief, a turning away. It is the war or part of it, merely a different sector of the field."

9 WCW is thinking of a jazz student from Pittsburgh named William Russell who "deserves most of the credit for the finding of Bunk," according to the notes by Eugene *Williams* on the sleeve of Commodore Records "Bunk Johnson's Jazz Band," a recording made in 1942 that WCW probably owned. According to Williams's letters, he also read about Willie "Bunk" Johnson in Fred Miller's essay in *The New Republic* (October 22, 1945), which mentions both William Russell and Eugene Williams, and in *Time* (November 5, 1945), which says, "A Pittsburgh jazz fan found him." WCW planned to hear Johnson in New York on September 28, 1945, but he missed that date and heard Bunk later on November 23, 1945.

10 Stevens used this poem as an epigraph for his "Nuances of a Theme by Williams," 1918.

[11] *The Oxford Book of American Verse,* ed., F. O. Matthiessen, 1950.

[12] The previous Sunday, June 11, 1950, *The New York Times Book Review* under the caption, "Headliners and Best Sellers" printed photographs of Williams, Hemingway, John O'Hara, Langston Hughes, Nelson Algren, Margaret Coit, and others, with the comment: "Here are a dozen writers . . . who for a variety of reasons are making news in the literary world this year." Near the beginning of the year, the Book Review of January 14 contained "Talk with W. C. Williams by Harvey Breit."

II–Dialogues

Notes by Linda Wagner

[1] Wallace Stevens used the term "anti-poetic" to praise Williams's poetry in his introduction to Williams's *Collected Poems* (1930), and Williams never forgave him for what he assumed was derogation.

[2] Williams refers here to the Prologue to his 1920 impressionistic *Kora in Hell: Improvisations,* probably written in 1918 (such slips in chronology are characteristic of Williams, but the tie with the Prologue probably is important because in it he opts for innovation, using Duchamp, Arensberg, Stevens's comments on freshness, and various examples of "the new" in all kinds of art forms).

[3] While Williams uses the term *story* to refer to his fiction–both long and short forms–he is here describing his use of character and incident in *Paterson.* Something of the dramatist, however, remains in whatever Williams does; and he seldom ever presents a character *per se;* characters are more often caught in the process of doing something, enacting their stories for the poet's observing eye.

[4] These lines were excerpted from the "Elena" section (II) of "Two Pendants: for the Ears," and the list is included as a list proper in the section of the poem, introduced by

> Listen, I said, I met a man
> last night told me what he'd brought
> home from the market:

Wallace's quotation robs the lines of their real significance in the poem, a genuine example of idiomatic speech. The poem is included in *The Collected Later Poems.*

[5] The phrase "literary nationalism" had been used in one segment of the *Partisan Review* question, and its connotation there was positive. The *PR* editors defined the term as being "a renewed emphasis, largely uncritical, on the specifically 'American' elements in our culture."

[6] Edgar Williams, the poet's brother.

[7] Mrs. Williams answered many of Koehler's questions during the interview for *Paris Review* because Williams's own speech–impaired after his several strokes–was not fluent enough to let him answer the questions easily.

Index